"How to Respond to an RFP"

Understanding the Bid and Proposal Process

First Edition

2010

Cover Artwork by Telesto Inc.,
300 Terry Fox Drive, Suite 100,
Kanata, Ontario
K2K 0E3

www.telesto.ca

Note for Librarians: A cataloguing record for this book is available from Library and Archives Canada at www.collectionscanada.gc.ca/amicus/index-e.html

ISBN: 978-0-9812055-5-7

Order this book online at **www.boreal.ca**

How to Respond to an RFP - Understanding the Bid and Proposal Process and most Boreal titles are available at major online book retailers.

Boreal Books
P.O. Box 4693 Postal Stn E,
Ottawa, Ontario
K1S 5H8

PREAMBLE

For over 30 years my career was focused on the world of procurement and the evaluation of complex bids for goods and services. During many years with the Government of Canada I was given cause to wonder why a firm would go to the often-heavy cost in time and dollars and operational disruptions to prepare a bid, only to lose it due to carelessness or a lack of understanding and expertise in the preparation of a bid.

This book is directed to those who wish to submit bids that give them the best possible chance of coming out a winner.

After retiring from the Government of Canada, I started training others and consulting on proposal writing for success. I soon found that there was a need for a text focusing on responding to both simple and complex RFPs. I had made extensive teaching notes over time in various formats, and used them to train others. I also relied heavily on my experience to fill in any gaps in my teaching notes.

When I decided to organize my notes, I found that there was enough material to fill two books. Therefore, two books, *Understanding the Bid and Proposal Process*; and *Winning Proposal Writing*.

Understanding the Bid and Proposal Process focuses on the various procurement documents that are in existence and the elements of the customer requirement and customer bid call processes.

Winning Proposal Writing focuses on what you must know and how to write your proposal in a highly-competitive environment.

To be successful, and not waste resources, you need to understand both the procurement process and what is expected from you, as a bidder, in each proposal.

I wish you, my reader, every success. It is said that "you can't win them all." The secret of success is to win your share or more.

Allan Cutler

Table of Contents

1. Introduction

Accepting the Reality

You may as well accept it. Proposal writing is here to stay. In fact, competitive bidding and the Request for Proposal process and procedures are becoming more and more complex. This book is a modern tool for firms who have to write proposals in bidding situations.

Although service (such as delivery requirements) enters into it, companies that primarily offer off-the-shelf goods are mainly evaluated by price. If this is your situation, this book is not designed for you. It is designed for companies who bid on services, or goods with a large service component and who are subject to quality evaluations based on the service component of their bid.

Over the last thirty-five years, I have been involved in reviewing many proposals. They ranged from simple written proposals of only a few thousand dollars to large, complex proposals that totalled multi-million dollars. The evaluation criteria applied to these written proposals have ranged from simple easy-to-understand criteria which were evaluated in one day, to extremely complex criteria which took weeks to evaluate and to complete.

Over and over again I saw firms make mistakes that should and could have been avoided. Sometimes these were omissions due to oversights; sometimes factual errors; sometimes instructions were ignored and sometimes it was apparent that the firms simply could not or did not understand the instructions.

More than once, I witnessed bids received as the result of a Request for Proposal where the total cost of preparing the proposal for each of the firms who bid was greater than the value of the final contract.

As an example, let's assume that you have bid on a requirement worth $60,000 and it cost you $5,000 to produce your proposal. In this case you find out that there were fourteen other bidders. This seriously reduces the chances of winning the bid for any one firm.

Assuming the other fourteen bidders have spent the same amount of money ($5,000) to prepare their bid, there is the following financial comparison. Total contract: $60,000. Total proposal cost: 15 firms x $5,000 each = $75,000.

Spending more money in preparing bids than the value of the final contract makes no financial sense. Obviously none of the firms had evaluated their odds of success. In other words they had not done a Bid/No Bid analysis.

I also observed a multi-million dollar bid where the firm forgot to enclose one critical document. There was another bid that had critical pages omitted due to poor or careless assembly of the proposal. There was still another bid where information was duplicated and placed in two sections – once in the correct spot and once replacing information that should have appeared. In the latter case, the information that should have been there was critical to the evaluation.

It became apparent to me that there is a need to help bidders improve their practices and procedures with regard to Request for Proposals. They need to understand the procurement process, the different documents and the different approaches to evaluation in order to increase their odds of success.

Setting the Scene

Proposal preparation includes a large component of risk management. Carefully undertaking the preparation will reduce the risk of failure and increase the probability of winning a bid.

Often, it is difficult to find and employ people who can write well and who also enjoy the challenge of proposal writing. Think about it from the viewpoint of these writers. There is considerable pressure on them. If too many proposals are lost, there could be a reduction in the company's workload. This could result in layoffs.

The proposal writer will not be the one laid off. After all, the writer is needed to win future proposals. However, the executives and the people laid off may well blame the writer. They may think, "If only the writer had done the job better, I would still have a job!" On the other hand, winning proposals does not necessarily mean the writer gets credit. This is a situation where the prevailing attitude could be, "We win but you lose?!" The attitude could also be, "We won! What did you do?'

If you are like most companies, proposal preparation and writing are not the skills or specialties that you offer to your customers. Just as you expect customers to contract with you for your specialized skills, you should consider hiring firms who specialize in preparing proposals.

Every customer is different. Although they try to define their specific requirements, many are not able to write a clear definition of what is required. This makes every bid document unique and requires each one to be read carefully. Often, if they are not written well, you, as a bidder, are left trying to interpret the bid yourself.

Care needs to be taken in writing a proposal. Successful

proposals will be used as a benchmark in any subsequent negotiations. Any and all commitments made in your proposals are legally binding and you will be expected to honour and fulfill them should you be awarded the contract.

Electronic Tendering

Over the last twenty years there has been a gradual evolution in how suppliers are sourced. Traditionally, companies and organizations used to create and maintain source lists for requirements. When a good or service was needed, bids documents were sent to these pre-selected bidders.

With the advent of the internet, a major change was started. In the normal course of events, private industry is the innovator and, once the innovation was established, the public sector followed. This time, that was not the case. The public sector was primarily responsible for the development of electronic tendering boards.

Electronic tendering enables every company to be aware of potential opportunities for bidding. Governments and other organizations post new requirements daily. The electronic tendering boards have removed, from the purchasing organization, the burden of identifying and selecting qualifying firms. Instead of the organization maintaining sources lists, it is a bidder self-selecting process. It is now the responsibility of each potential bidder to determine if it meets the specifications of the RFP and to determine if it wants to bid.

Although the main users of electronic tendering are public procurement organizations, the private industry occasionally uses them as well. The reason for the difference is that the public sector is accountable to a "public". The public sector is aware that it can challenged regarding fairness of the process and the resulting contract. The private sector concentrates more on relationship building.

Electronic bidding has caused major changes in how bidding is done. Now, public sector organizations spend more time writing detailed statements of requirement and developing evaluation criteria. More than ever, it is necessary to be precise, detailed and unbiased. Evaluators want to ensure that they will have a manageable number of qualifying bids to evaluate. Compliance with the RFP criteria is strictly enforced.

With the precision and increased degree of complexity shown in the bid documents, companies need to read and analyze the documents more closely. A decision as to whether the company should bid (Bid/No Bid Decision) needs to be done.

With a source list, it was easier for a qualified bidder to assess the odds. You knew that the bidding was done to a restricted list. Although electronic tendering can allow companies to see who else is interested and who has downloaded the RFP, this information is not provided in all cases. Even when you know who has obtained a copy of the bid document, it may be difficult to determine how many will bid. As a result, as previously mentioned, the situation occurs where the combined cost of preparing proposals by all bidders is greater than the value of the subsequent contract.

.

2. The Bid Process

The Procurement Process

Procurement is simply a process of systematically going from point A to point B and ending at point Z. Within this process, there are many twists and turns. To understand these variations, it is first necessary to understand the process.

The procurement process is a much larger concept than the bid process but the terminology is often used interchangeably. Generally, the procurement process can be divided into four stages:

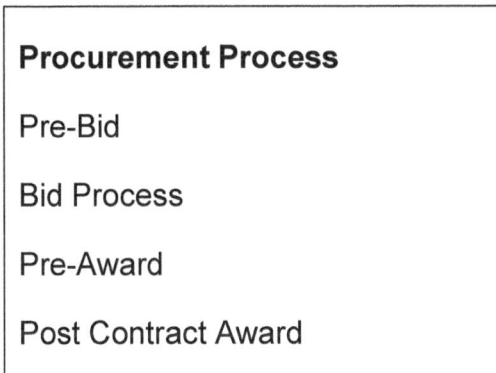

> **Procurement Process**
>
> Pre-Bid
>
> Bid Process
>
> Pre-Award
>
> Post Contract Award

Pre-Bid: All activities by the purchaser from initial conception of the need, through to writing the requirement definition, to creating the final bid document with appropriate evaluation criteria.

Bid Process: All activities from the release of the RFP. This includes the Bid/No Bid decision and the drafting of the proposal. It also includes all events that take place up to the bid closing date, including the submission of the bid.

Pre-Award: All activities from the time that the bid has closed through evaluation, recommendation and the actual award of the contract.

Post Contract Award: All activities from the time that the contract was awarded. This includes contract administration and necessary amendments until the final completion of the contract.

Although the procurement process starts long before the actual bidding situation and doesn't end until the contract is completed and payment made, this book focuses primarily on the Bidding Process. This is the element of the procurement process that needs to be understood if a bidder is to be successful.

However, there are also elements of the Pre-Award and Post Contract Award periods which may have an impact on a bidder. These are included in the bid process for convenience. For example, Debriefings, which are a Post Contract Award situation, are included in this section.

The Bid Process

An understanding of both the competitive and non-competitive bid process is critical if you are to bid successfully.

While the major steps of the process are listed below, it is helpful to list them and then discuss them in more depth. The listing is essentially in the chronological order that they occur in the process but this is not always the case. Some overlap, some are simultaneous and some occur throughout the complete bid process. Furthermore, not all steps are necessary all the time.

As the procurement becomes more complex, the process also becomes more complex. The result is that more steps need to be included.

The Bid Process:
The Bid Release
Bid/No Bid Decision
Commencement
Red Team Review
Production of Proposal
Questions and Answers
Bidders' Conference, Site Visits
Amendments
Submission
Bid Extensions
Oral Presentations/Demonstrations
Debriefings

The Bid Release

Once the RFP has been released, the bid process has started. The clock starts ticking. The RFP will have a closing date, time and location for proposal submission. It helps if you think of the time element of the bid process as a ticking clock that has the alarm set (bid closing time). It is going to go off whether the proposal is done or not. Can you hear it? Tick...Tick...Tick...

Every hour lost is an hour less that you have to work on your proposal. Therefore, you should be watching every day or on a regular schedule for bid opportunities that are of interest to you and are posted on the electronic bulletin boards. Time lost can never be regained.

Many firms check the electronic procurement bulletin boards daily. As soon as they see a potential bid opportunity they immediately obtain a copy of the RFP. The next thing they do is to look at the closing date. Based on the closing date, they may make a decision that there is plenty of time and put the bid aside.

Their attitude is, "Why should I look at the RFP? There is plenty of time and I have more important work to do." They continue to work on what they believe to be "more important and urgent work".

This is a misconception. It reveals a lack of understanding of the situation. As soon as you obtain the RFP, you should start working on it. There is always an "excuse" not to do something promptly.

There could be major problems (from your perspective) in the bid documents. For example, the Statement of Work may contain proprietary references that would preclude you from bidding. The Statement of Work may also cause you difficulties in sourcing materials and sub-contractors through unnecessary and restrictive technical specifications. Waiting to start working on the RFP may result in an inability to request or make changes.

Sometimes, even a minor adjustment to the evaluation criteria, the Statement of Work or a time requirement in an RFP will correct the situation. From screened out and not able to bid, a firm becomes screened in. A potentially lucrative contract opportunity can be lost by delaying the review. You cannot rely on other firms having the same problems.

Review the RFP right away.

The Bid/No Bid Decision

This is a critical step in the process and the first decision point. It will be discussed in more detail later. With RFPs becoming more and more complex, preparing a proposal has become a very costly exercise. While the expense is relative to the size of the company, the cost for all companies has increased. On extremely high dollar value and complex bids, some proposals have cost over $1M to prepare.

This decision includes the people cost and other proposal preparation expenses. No firm wants to spend time and money unnecessarily. Many factors need to be carefully considered and these factors are different for every firm and every bid.

The critical examination of the RFP will aid in making this decision.

Commencement – Getting Started

Having decided to bid, it is critical to start working on the proposal. Many firms have only one or two people preparing proposals so no meeting is necessary. A simple discussion may be all that is required.

If the bid is extremely complex and requires the commitment of many people, you should have a pre-planning meeting of everyone. If you are working in different locations, this can be done by a teleconference.

This meeting determines:

* What needs to be written and by whom,
* The total time that will be necessary to produce a proposal,
* The time commitment and priority that must be made by every person involved

Regardless of the number of people involved, good planning requires that a time line be created. The clock is ticking; there are many things to be done; you have to know that you are on schedule to complete the proposal before time runs out.

An examination of the RFP (to be discussed in more detail later) will usually reveal that there are unanswered questions, contradictions or information gaps that need to be addressed.

Start writing the response immediately. Work on the sections that you can quickly begin with. If possible, create outlines for the other sections. Keep that ticking clock in mind. Written responses can be more readily revised and improved if work drafting the proposal has commenced.

Red Team Review

The Red Team Review is responsible for quality assurance and proposal improvement. It is a process that runs parallel to the development of the written proposal. Its work focuses on analyzing two important criteria – the RFP, and the proposal that is being prepared in response to the RFP.

The first step is a critical evaluation of the RFP in order to understand the bid. The Red Team watches for missing items, conflicting information, gaps in information and incorrect evaluation criteria. Second, it reviews the draft proposal. Drafts are not normally completed all at once but in sections.

Do not wait until everything is completed. Have the Red Team review the drafts as each section is produced. Time is of the essence (the ticking clock, remember) and it is possible to wait too long to be able to locate and correct written errors.

The Red Team reviews each section and looks for consistency between sections. Suggestions will also be given to the Proposal Manager regarding improvements to the proposal. Questions may be raised that need to be sent to the procurement organization regarding clarification of the RFP.

To work properly, the Red Team requires time. Their review should never be rushed. Reviews done at the last minute are less effective and more prone to error and omissions.

It is also important to note that a proper Red Team does not participate in writing the proposal. The old saying applies, "You can't review your own work."

The Bid Process

Production of Proposal

It is preferable to structure and to produce the proposal in sections so that last minute changes can be made. In this way, some sections are finalized before others.

However, time must be allowed to verify that all sections of the proposal are written in the same format, have consistent information and there are no apparent contradictions.

It is also necessary to allow time for the final preparation and production of the proposal. This includes the last edit to ensure consistency throughout the bid and the time needed to produce the number of copies required for delivery to the customer.

If the proposal has been properly prepared in sections, it can be produced on separate photocopiers or printers and assembled. Time has to be allowed for this production and assembly as accidents can and do happen. Pages can get stuck together, sometimes with serious consequences.

Sections can be wrongly assembled, again with possible serious consequences.

In one large RFP, a firm submitted their proposal but, due to a photocopier jam, four pages of pricing were missing. They had not sent the original proposal which had the missing pages. None of the copies had the missing pages. On this basis they lost a large bid. The owner of the firm learned what had happened during a debriefing regarding losing the bid. I subsequently learned that he fired the employee responsible.

Questions and Answers

"Q and A" as it is commonly referred to, can be asked throughout the complete bid process. As a result of the initial review of the RFP, there may be questions that need to be answered to clarify corrections and contradictory information.

Generally, questions can only be addressed to the Procurement Officer in charge of the RFP.

Further questions will be identified as the bidding time continues. In fact, published answers to questions earlier asked by your firm or other firms can easily result in further questions. The answers may cause complications. They may contradict other answers already given or even the original RFP.

Clarity prevents misunderstandings. If you don't understand or something appears misleading, ask a question.

Bidders' Conference, Site Visit

A Bidders' Conference or Site Visit is held during the bid period in order to ensure that all potential bidders have an understanding of the requirement. Normally, it is not the dollar value of the requirement that determines whether these are held. It is the complexity or sensitivity (possibly political) of the requirement.

During either of these events, bidders have the opportunity to ask for clarifications and further information. This is in addition to, and does not replace, the written questions that can also be asked during the process.

The difference between a Bidders' Conference and Site Visit is fairly easy to describe. A Bidders' Conference is held in a meeting room and is, in fact, a formal meeting. On the other hand, a Site Visit is a tour of the facilities where the work will take place. Bidders get to see exactly what is required to be done and the space available to work in. This increases their understanding of the requirement.

Attendance at either of these may be optional (ie. you can still bid whether you attend or not). Bidders should always attend. Attending will help you identify your competition and/or firms that could be approached for a strategic alliance or joint venture in submitting a bid. You may also hear information conveyed that is not subsequently provided to the bidders in writing.

Amendments

Amendments to the bid document occur for many reasons. For example, they may be the result of questions raised and answers given regarding the bidding information. They may also be used to correct errors, oversights and contradictions in the original RFP.

Complex RFPs by their nature seem to require more amendments. As a result, it is normal for a complex RFP to provide for an extension in bidding time. However, you should not depend on this when preparing your proposal

In the event of Site Visits and/or Bidders' Conferences, it is becoming common to issue the minutes of the Site Visit or Bidders' Conference as an amendment to the RFP. When this occurs, it is necessary to closely read and examine the minutes to filter out the changes to the RFP that have been approved. You also want to ensure the written minutes reflect your understanding of what was said at the Site Visit or Bidders' Conference.

Submission

Competitive bids normally have a common closing time. It is important to ensure that your proposal is submitted on time. Accidents have been known to happen.

Allow time for problems in delivery. Remember that the old expression is true, "Accidents can be prevented." Yet, accidents still happen. As an example, a bidder was driving to deliver his bid at the last minute and not only was traffic exceptionally heavy but he also had a flat tire. Needless to say, he delivered the bid late and was disqualified.

Normally a bidder is requested to submit more than one copy of the bid. Should the bid be of sufficient monetary value, it is recommended that the copies be split and two separate deliveries be arranged. In this way, if one has an unavoidable delay, the other delivery will still be on time. The delivery that is late will be deemed a confirmation of the bid (since the other part arrived on time) and the firm will have met the bid closing requirements.

Bid Extensions

In complex RFP situations, it is normal for bid extensions to occur. This can be very disruptive in proposal planning if you are not prepared for it. The answers to complex questions may require significant changes, the consequence being a bid extension.

This is, unfortunately, a circular and unavoidable dilemma. A bid extension causes disruption. The disruption causes a question. The question causes an answer to be given. The answer causes another bid extension. The bid extension causes another disruption. The disruption causes a question. ...and so on...

Many questions requiring many answers equal many amendments. Time may be required by all parties (the bidders and the issuer of the RFP) to incorporate the changes.

It is also not wise to anticipate the length of a bid extension. Often they may be only a few days when you are expecting a couple of weeks. Monitor all changes to the RFP. Extensions normally mean changes not only in the RFP but changes to be incorporated properly in your proposal.

The Bid Process

Oral Presentations/Demonstrations

It is normal practice in a complex procurement for the customer to want a proposal explained in more depth. For this reason, an RFP may require an oral presentation. The oral presentation takes place after the customer has completed the written evaluation of the bids but before final decisions have been made. The oral presentation will be evaluated. However, only those firms with a written proposal that qualified will be invited to give an oral presentation.

Oral presentations usually have a specific time period that cannot be exceeded and a formal structure for the presentation that is common to all bidders. This is an opportunity for the bidder to expand on the proposal, explaining key elements in more detail. In private industry, the oral presentation is generally considered more important than it is in the public sector.

Normally new information can not be introduced but existing information can be clarified. A firm skilled in "clarification" will have an advantage.

In preparing for the oral presentation, firms should undertake a rehearsal. Assign a person with a stopwatch to time the presentation and act as an observer. The Red Team could be used for this. This person will be able to offer suggestions for improvement. By this means, you will have the opportunity to find glitches and to eliminate problems. A highly professional presentation can then be developed.

Debriefings

Whether you win or lose the bid, you should request a debriefing. As the losing firm, you want to know where you made errors and how to avoid them in the future. As the winning firm, you want to know how to improve your bid in the future.

How to Respond to a RFP
Understanding the Bid and Proposal Process

3. Bid Documents

There are several different types of bid documents. Additionally, the titles of the bid documents change depending on the preferences of the public sector organization or the private industry firm that issued the bid.

Everyone, it seems has the right to its own jargon. There is no standard although many firms, agencies and institutions use similar terminology. The two most common terms used are the Request for Information and the Request for Proposal, which will be discussed in more depth later.

For simplicity, the following are groupings that reflect the purpose of the bidding opportunity. There also follows a series of definitions and explanations. It is important when in doubt to read the definition and apply it as appropriate.

Definitions and Explanations

A. Pre-Bidding

Request for Information (RFI)

A Request for Information is a means of collecting information and is used when a company or government is exploring the possibility or feasibility of procurement.

Advance Notice

As the name indicates, it gives notice to all interested firms that a bid will be coming in the near future. This allows firms to prepare themselves for the opportunity.

Prequalification (Source list, bid opportunity)

This is a form of restricting the actual bidding to only those firms who are interested. With the advent of electronic bidding, this has become less common.

B. Sole Source/Negotiated Requirement

ACAN (Advance Contract Award Notice)

This announces the intention to negotiate a contract with only one firm. This announcement is generally used in the public sector, not private industry, due to the requirement of openness and transparency. It gives the opportunity for the purchaser to find out if there are competitors in the industry instead of dealing with only one firm.

C. Competitive Bids

Telephone buy (T-buy)

Telephone buys are designed for small-dollar value competitive purchases. They are normally easy to describe on the phone and may or may not be required urgently. Normally the bidding is restricted to firms already known to the buyer and the evaluation is strictly on price. Due to the low dollar value, minimum documentation is required. The buyer normally receives the bids. This is commonly called "desk closing".

In the past, buyers and sellers used to rely on bid information given and received over the phone. With e-mail readily available, the T-buy method is no longer commonly used.

Request for Quotation (RFQ)

RFQs are also designed for small dollar value competitive purchases. It has almost completely replaced telephone buys.

Bid Documents

RFQs are used in lieu of lengthy formal RFP documentation.

Bid documents are sent and received in written form, normally by e-mail or fax. Due to the low risk in procurement, the bid documents are simplified so that contracting decisions can be done quickly.

Invitation to Tender (ITT)

ITTs are used for higher dollar value where the requirements are easy to define. They are most commonly used in procurement of goods (such as commercially available products) and rarely used in the procurement of services.

These requirements are normally posted on the electronic bidding boards, the bids assessed and awarded by price.

The evaluation is normally done by price with the lowest priced responsive bid being awarded the contract.

Request for Proposal (RFP)

RFPs are used for higher dollar value requirements where the requirement is not easily defined and where there is room for interpretation or misunderstanding. They are most commonly used in procurement of services where a supplier cannot be chosen solely on the basis of price.

The evaluation is normally done by a blend of quality and price with the best value, as defined, being awarded the contract. There are many different ways of doing this.

Similar terms are used for the same purpose instead of Request for Proposal such as "Request to Bid", "Invitation to Bid", etc. However, Request for Proposal is the most common term and, consequently, the term used in this book to describe the bid document.

How to Respond to a RFP
Understanding the Bid and Proposal Process

Request for Standing Offer (RFSO)

Standing Offers are used for large dollar value repetitive competitive purchases where either the requirement or the elements of the requirement can be defined. RFSOs may be used with either goods or services and there is no guarantee of usage.

The evaluation may be done on price or a blend of quality and price with a Standing Offer being authorized. A contract is formed only when a call-up is issued against the Standing Offer.

Request for Supply Arrangement (RFSA)

Supply Arrangements are used for large dollar value repetitive competitive purchases where the requirement can only be defined generally and there is no guarantee of usage.

RFSAs are used for procurement of services. The evaluation may be done on price or a blend of quality and price with a Supply Arrangement being authorized. When there is a requirement, only pre-qualified Supply Arrangement vendors may be given an opportunity to compete for the requirement. This speeds up the procurement processing time.

4. Request for Information (RFI)

As already defined, a Request for Information is a means of collecting information and is used when a private industry company, or public sector organization or government, is exploring the possibility or feasibility of procurement. They are not taking bids at this stage.

To properly understand the Request for Information, it is necessary to look at the demand from two viewpoints – the end user (the people who want the information) and the potential bidder (firms interested in providing the service).

From the viewpoint of the end user

From the end user vantage, the Request for Information is a tool to collect information and ideas in a coordinated fashion from all potential suppliers at the same time. In complex bidding, this is an excellent preplanning tool for preparing a future bid.

A RFI can also be used to find out availability of products or services. Often the nature and scope of product or service availability is unknown. The RFI allows the end user to review new products, services or ideas in the marketplace that he/she may not be aware of. It may also serve as an alert regarding resources (people, funding, etc) that will be needed for the proposed requirement.

In these cases, the question being asked is, "Can we do what we what to do or do we have to make changes?" Once the market has been canvassed, a bid document can be prepared. Another question being asked may be, "Is there competition in the industry or only one source of supply?"

It may allow the end user to make an initial assessment of the possibility of a valuable and viable competition. Although not all firms have the time to respond in detail to a "Request" in contrast to a "Bid", usually firms have time to indicate if they would be interested in bidding on the actual requirement.

From the viewpoint of the firm

From the viewpoint of your firm, a Request for Information has many attractions. Responding, at a minimum, is an expression of interest in the customer's requirement.

An RFI is the advance notice of the potential procurement. This creates an opportunity for your firm to suggest improvements or innovations with regard to the Statement of Work (Requirement). This could include, technical improvements, pricing mechanisms, duration of contract, methodologies and professional expertise required.

Through suggestions, changes may be made that would result in a competitive advantage or proprietary requirements in the resulting RFP. This is to the future advantage of a potential bidder as it can create a more level playing field for bidding. At a minimum, it represents the opportunity to remove inadvertent biases that have already been written in the RFI.

Responding with recommendations demonstrates to a potential client that the firm is capable and qualified. The downside to offering suggestions are that they are not chargeable (ie. they are offered free) and the suggestions, if used, will be available to all bidders in the future.

Normally, it is not a requirement that you have to respond if you want to bid on the future bid. However, there are always exceptions. By responding, you protect your future ability to bid on the actual requirement.

Request for Information (RFI)

In the event that you do not have the time or available resources to respond fully, it is still recommended that you submit a letter stating your interest. In this way, the end user is aware that there are potential bidders and that there can be a competitive bid.

With the development of electronic bidding, it is now very rare (if ever) for a Request for Information to state that a bidder must respond if they want to respond to the future RFP. However, should this be a requirement, the RFI will state this.

5. Sole Source Contracts

Sole Source Contracts

There are two separate elements that are of significance in sole sourcing a contract. The first element is the reason for sole sourcing. The second element is why they chose your firm.

Every public sector organization and every private industry firm has a different process for sole sourcing. However, the reasons generally fall within the same categories.

As the federal government is Canada's largest purchaser of goods and services, sole sourcing will be examined from its perspective. The process it uses will be described, including the challenge mechanism available for other interested suppliers.

Notwithstanding the above, it is important to keep in mind that almost all organizations using the electronic bidding board system have similar procedures.

ACAN (Advance Contract Award Notice)

The federal government uses ACANs to notify potential bidders of its intention to sole source a requirement. This is a relatively recent innovation and its implementation coincides with the introduction of electronic bidding.

Electronic bidding has changed the landscape of procurement. No longer is it necessary to keep a list of potential sources. Instead, all firms can review bids and determine for themselves if they should bid. While this has increased the number of potential bidders, it has also decreased the knowledge of alternate sources of supply for some procurement initiatives. ACANs were created to address this gap in knowledge.

An ACAN is published to advise all firms of a potential bid opportunity where it is proposed to contract with only one source of supply. This allows potential bidders to know of the requirement and also gives them the opportunity to challenge the rationale for sole sourcing. In this way they can ensure that they are given an opportunity to bid on providing the good or service. From the federal government's viewpoint this is an advantage as they learn of potential competition in a market where they believed that there was only one qualified supplier.

Why Sole Source?

The following explanation is focused on the federal government rationales but it is important to note that other public sector organizations also publish ACANs. Their guidelines, while different, have essentially the same rationales.

According to the federal policy, there are only four acceptable reasons for ACANs: Urgency/Emergency, Low Dollar Value, Not in the Public Interest to Solicit Bids, and Only One Supplier.

Urgency

Urgency is defined as a pressing emergency where delays in taking action would be injurious to the public interest. These are unavoidable circumstances that require immediate action. Floods, forest fires or ice storms are some examples of urgency. Without immediate action there could be loss of life, extensive environmental or other damage. There is no time for formal bids and immediate decisions are required as to the source of supply.

Poor planning is not considered a valid reason for urgency. Therefore, delays caused by development of the technical specification, evaluation criteria, the RFP, etc. cannot be used as rationale for urgency.

Sole Source Contracts

Note:

Other public sector and private industry firms may classify this rationale as "emergency" instead of "urgency". The critical issue is whether delay would be harmful. Private industry may include a business imperative as an urgency for sole sourcing. It would be harmful to the continued success or survival of the private sector firm.

Low Dollar Value

With a few exceptions, the federal government defines low dollar value as situations where the estimated expenditure does not exceed $25,000, taxes included. A notable exception is $100,000 or less, GST included, for "architectural, engineering and other services in respect of the planning, design, preparation or supervision of the construction, repair, renovation or restoration of a work."

Note:

Low dollar value is a common justification for sole source contracts in either the private industry or the public sector. This represents an opportunity to obtain significant work for firms who do not have proprietary rights on a product or service. Small contracts can, and do, add up and small contracts can lead to large opportunities.

Not in Public Interest to Solicit Bids

These are procurements where there are security issues and other considerations. Alternately, there may be a need to alleviate some socio-economic disparity or to preserve a specialized source of supply to ensure that the future needs of Canadians will be addressed. Of the four rationales (urgency, low dollar value, not in the public interest and only one supplier) this is the vaguest justification. It is also the justification that may cause political problems so it is the least used.

The use of "Not in the Public Interest to Solicit Bids" is more common at the federal level. However, it is used in other public sector organizations, for example, in procurement of police surveillance or security work. It is rarely, if ever, used in private industry.

Only One Supplier

This is another common justification used for posting an ACAN. Situations where there are only one supplier are relatively easy to define. There are cases where only one firm or supplier is capable of performing the contract. There may be a technical issue, for example, compatible parts that interconnect with existing equipment. There are also situations where patent or copyright requirements preclude competition. Finally, in a few cases, there may be specialized knowledge or expertise that can only be obtained from one firm.

There is a problem with this justification. Although an undesirable and incorrect practice, it is often used when the proposed contractor is the only one known to the client, as a means of avoiding competition.

Note:

This justification is used equally by the public sector and private industry when there are issues of copyright requirements or unique technological expertise. The use of Microsoft Word is an example of only one supplier as it is covered by copyright requirements. However, there is a difference between buying the product and leasing rights to its use. Buying MS Word is a situation where there is only one supplier but there are many agents who can provide the package. Leasing the rights to the use of MSWord for multiple users probably means negotiation direct with Microsoft.

Challenging ACANs

ACANs can be challenged, but only by firms who could potentially bid. This is the fundamental weakness in the system and leaves the use of ACANs open to abuse.

Even if an expert sees that the wrong rationale was used, it is difficult to challenge the ACAN. Only a firm who could bid is allowed to initiate a challenge and they have the burden of proof to overcome. As a result, very few challenges succeed.

As a potential bidder, before proceeding to challenge an ACAN you have to consider both whether the justification for the challenge is valid and if you are able to provide sound substantiation for the challenge.

The decision tree is simple. It is referred to as "Could you? Should you?"

> *Could you?*
>
> *Should you?*

"Could you?" This first question is straightforward. Are you able to supply the service or good that they propose to buy from a single source? This involves examining the requirements and the justification used for the ACAN.

If you can challenge, the second part is "Should you?" The second question is more sensitive. Some ACANS, for example, are for services provided by the Salvation Army, The Red Cross or other recognized charitable organizations. In these cases you have to decide if you should challenge, recognizing the political downside and potential negative publicity. You could be perceived as trying to take work away from a charitable organization so that you can make a profit.

Examples of critical elements of ACANs are at the end of this section. Examples of ACANS written in full along with an analysis of their merits are included in Appendix A

How a Sole Source Firm is Selected

In a "sole source" situation (ie. non-competitive), buyers are often able to use his/her discretion. They have to decide which supplier will receive the business. The question that you need to answer is, "Why should they choose your firm?"

If you are like most firms, you do not have proprietary rights on a product or service. Therefore, it is important for you to understand how you can create the situation to ensure that your firm will be considered for sole source contracts.

Buyers normally choose firms with the following characteristics:

- The firm has a solid and well-known professional and business reputation.
- The firm is well known for producing high quality work.
- The pricing structure of the firm is considered fair.
- The firm has done previous work for the buyer.
- The firm has established trust in relation to offering fair prices and value for the dollar.

It is evident that there is a commonality in the above characteristics— relationship and reputation building.

Relationship building is a prerequisite for many such opportunities. A firm many or may not have an existing relationship as a supplier. Regardless, keeping in touch with the buyer on a regular basis will help open up these opportunities. This contact need not be frequent but it must be maintained at appropriate intervals.

This applies equally to the public sector where they have limited opportunity to award contracts to preferred suppliers. When the opportunity presents itself and the rules/regulations can still be respected, they will select firms that provide them with a high level of comfort. In other words, firms that they have a relationship with.

ACAN Examples

It is worth examining several ACANs to see the reasoning used. Annex A has more ACANs reproduced in their entirety as it is important that you be familiar with the form and wording used in the complete ACAN. This will enable your analysis to be done more quickly and to be more complete.

However, for illustration purposes at this point the complete ACAN is not necessary. The following are actual excerpts from ACANs. The critical element from a bidder's viewpoint is the justification used to sole source.

Example ACAN #1

"We believe that this person is the only individual in British Columbia who possess the qualifications outlined above and is available and willing to provide the services required within ABC public organization in the Pacific Region."

Note:

The justification for this ACAN appears to be Only One Supplier. This should not have been an ACAN. An ACAN appears to have been used as a means of avoiding competition. The buyer has no knowledge to support the premise of only one source of supply. No reason is actually given as to why this person is the only one who has the qualifications. Others may have them and be available and the justification acknowledges this when it says, "we believe..."

Only possible suppliers can challenge the ACAN. Many firms are reluctant to do so. They worry about retaliation in the form of receiving unfavourable evaluation scores in future RFPs.

Example ACAN #2

"It is proposed to award this contract, for a value of $xxx. to XYZ. The proposed Contractor holds the intellectual property rights to the required software."

Note:

The justification for this ACAN is Only One Supplier. In this case the ACAN is justified as the firm in questions owns the intellectual property right to the software.

Example ACAN #3

"XYZ Resource Society currently provides community-based residential facility services for women. Continuity of a qualified service provider is necessary to ensure risk management is effectively monitored."

Note:

Similar to ACAN #1 the justification for this ACAN appears, on the surface, to be Only One Supplier. As with ACAN #1, this should not have been an ACAN and has been used as a means of avoiding competition. This particular ACAN is fairly easy to challenge as the only justification is "continuity", which is not a valid reason.

Sole Source Contracts

This is an example of a "Could you? Should you?" decision. Knowing that you can challenge, you are faced with a "Should you" decision. A Society is normally non-profit. There could be a negative impact on your business from resulting publicity should your challenge become known.

Example ACAN #4

"...has determined that XYZ is uniquely qualified to fulfill the requirement and possesses expansive knowledge, the necessary experience and technical expertise and is considered to be the only qualified supplier to perform this contract given their rare combination of skills and expertise. XYZ is comprised of PhD level experts in public health practice, health economics, systems analysis and health information science." Note:

The justification for this ACAN appears again to be Only One Supplier. Due to the complexity of the language used, it is more difficult to be certain if the ACAN is valid.

The major indicator that there may be a problem with the justification is the start "...has determined that XYZ is uniquely qualified..." They are not stating that there is only one source of supply; they are stating that it is their opinion that there is one source of supply

6. Competitive Bidding

Why do Firms Bid in a Competitive Environment?

When asked, firms state that the reasons that they bid are to increase their business, for more profit or for other reasons such as to increase their market share or to enter a new market. What they don't realize is that there is an underlying set of ethical principles involved in their bidding – Equality of Treatment and the Integrity of the Bid Process.

These two principles are the foundations of competitive procurement. Unless these ethical principles are maintained firms will not bid. Why would a firm waste costly time and resources preparing an expensive proposal if they believe that the winner of the bid is already determined?

Equality of Treatment

This is the principle of fairness. With a competitive bid, the expectation is that there will be equality with regard to the opportunity to win. This means that the same information will be provided to all potential bidders at the same time. No one firm will be deliberately given information to help them win over others.

For the evaluation, all bidders will be evaluated equally based on the same criteria. Bias will be eliminated by not allowing previous knowledge or relationships with the customer to be assessed. In this way, new firms have an opportunity to enter the market and compete successfully.

In the rare event that previous experience is to be assessed, this is identified clearly in the RFP rated criteria, along with information as to how this is to be evaluated.

Integrity of the Bid Process

This is the principle of trust. Mechanisms are set up to ensure that the process maintains its integrity. Bids are closed at a common location and at the same time in a secure location. In this way, any information contained in a bid that, if known, may provide an advantage to other bidders, remains confidential until the bids are opened. No one sees what has been bid until after the closing time. From a buyer's perspective, it minimizes accusations of bid rigging and virtually ensures his/her integrity will not be questioned.

The Three Main Bid Documents

In the competitive bidding environment for large service contracts, there are three main bidding tools – Request for Proposal, Request for Standing Offer and Request for Supply Arrangement. Goods with a large service component use Request for Proposal or Request for Standing Offer. The Request for Supply Arrangement is not well suited to goods procurement.

It is important to realize the distinction between the three main bidding documents. While the procurement process is similar, there are important implications for the successful firm that vary according to the bid methodology. For practical purposes, from a bidder's perspective, the three main bidding tools are the same. As long as the requirement is complex and calls for a complex assessment methodology, each response will have a similar methodology.

Request for Proposal (RFP)

An RFP is a request to all bidders to submit a detailed response (proposal) to complex requirements. Bidders are to submit proposals to ensure that the service can be successfully provided by them. The proposal is an offer against definite requirements. The final contract will state words to the effect, "Your Proposal is Accepted." This creates a legally binding contract.

Request for Standing Offer (RFSO)

A RFSO is a request to all bidders to submit offers. The final document will contain words to the effect, "Your offer is authorized.' No contract being created at this time. To create a contract, there must be both offer and acceptance. At the time of approval there is no acceptance, as there is no guarantee of any work of any amount. If and when there is work to be performed, a second document called a "call-up" will be issued. This call-up is acceptance of the Standing Offer.

Request for Supply Arrangement (RFSA)

A RFSA is the middle ground between an RFP (result = contract) and a RFSO (result = standing offer) for work. It is extremely versatile and can take many forms. The most common use results in a Supply Arrangement that binds the bidder to terms and conditions with regard to future opportunities for direct work. This is equivalent to a pre-qualified bidders list since all firms who meet the requirements will be authorized. Similar to a Standing Offer, there is no guarantee of work. However, should there be a requirement, the qualified suppliers will have an opportunity to bid on the requirement. This may be a Request for Proposal issued only to those firms who have qualified under the Request for Supply Arrangement.

Knowing the difference between the bid documents helps potential bidders understand the risk associated with the respective bid. Understanding this also helps in determining whether the costs of submitting a proposal are reasonable.

7. Request for Proposal

As already stated, depending on the firm or client and the bidding tool used, the name of the document may change. However, when discussing bidding, Request for Proposal is the most common term used to describe complex competitive bidding.

Based on the above definition, from now on RFP will be used as a generic sense term meaning a bid issued by a potential customer asking suppliers to bid for a specific project or service.

The RFP normally details the elements of a statement of work, the deliverables that are expected, the time frame for completion, the criteria for evaluation and acceptance. It also details the date and time when the bids will be open (deadline for responding). Depending on the situation, it may also include a date when the contract will be awarded.

Normally bids are not evaluated by a direct comparison between bids. However, RFP evaluations are designed to allow evaluators to make comparisons between bidders through a structured evaluation. This helps streamline the process of selecting the best one.

There are two main types of RFP.

The first and most common RFP type specifies the content and structure of the response (a proposal). It also gives strict guidelines for what will be evaluated. A variation on this RFP type simply states what is required. The content and formatting of the proposal is at the discretion of the bidder.

The second RFP type is far less common. It simply describes what is wanted and states the amount of the budget. The evaluation of the RFP is based on the maximum amount of goods or services that can be delivered or provided within this budget.

Overview – Bidding

While it is later described in more detail, an overview of some of the bid process elements is useful at this point.

Pre-determined evaluation criteria are described in the RFP. Firms are required to submit detailed written proposals to prove they can meet these criteria. A team of evaluators read and evaluate the proposals against the evaluation criteria. The evaluators meet and discuss their assessments, coming to a consensus score. The results are given to the procurement officer who factors in the evaluation results against the financial bids, using predetermined methodology. The successful firm is then determined.

RFPs can range from being very simple and straightforward to being very complicated and convoluted. With this wide degree of variation, the process can also vary widely. Only a few suppliers may be allowed to bid or the bidders may have to determine for themselves if they should bid.

To add another layer of complexity, within the bid process, RFPs can have many variations. Not all bid process elements are used on every bid. There can be site visits or bidders' conferences to explain the bid to all potential bidders and oral presentations where bidders can elaborate on their qualifications or explain their proposal more fully and demonstrate existing capabilities.

Regardless of the document or the details, each RFP must be responded to fully. If a format is given, the proposal must follow it and fit the format required. Careful verification must be done to ensure that no critical information is lost.

Request for Proposal

Keep in mind, that although the RFP process requires clients to put thought into project requirements, a poorly written RFP is not uncommon. This denotes a lack of either careful thought or knowledge by the client and could result in a failed bid.

Careful analysis of an RFP is a necessity. If you do not seek clarification and/or corrections you may have to write a proposal without a clear understanding of what is required, how you should respond or your proposal will be evaluated. However, having written it, clients will rely on the proposal as the most important and legitimate document when they have discussions with you.

Another consideration is the need to be careful in what you write. Should you be successful, the client will use your proposal during the subsequent negotiations for a contract and during the life of the project. What you write may remain with you for years, as many proposals are for long-term contracts.

8. Bid/No Bid Decision Making – The First Step

Should You Respond?

Management have to be aware that it is not necessary to respond to every bid opportunity. If asked, senior personnel will normally agree with the above statement. However, their actions speak louder than words. Faced with an opportunity to bid they often insist on trying, even against heavy odds.

What must be factored into the decision to bid is the knowledge that preparing a proposal in response to an RFP is extremely time consuming. The complete proposal and every element, while being prepared, must be checked, rechecked and re-rechecked. Failure to meet just one criteria that is defined as mandatory could easily disqualify a firm. Furthermore, failure to obtain the necessary score can disqualify a firm. Given these conditions, firms should not prepare a proposal without a reasonable chance of winning the bid.

Bidding for the sake of bidding is a mistake. It is far less expensive to submit a letter expressing your interest for future opportunities than it is to devote resources to a lost cause. There is also the opportunity cost that must be considered. Diverting your resources to prepare a proposal is a decision. It is a decision not to devote them to more productive and potentially profitable activities. Preparing a proposal, regardless of size, has a time and money cost. This is especially costly if your firm charges out employees on a per diem or hourly basis.

One significant and often overlooked opportunity cost is the growth of a business. If you are focusing on growth, you can't expand if you don't focus newer and larger requirements. This may mean passing up opportunities to bid on requirements that can easily be done by your firm. Bidding means committing resources. Committed resources limit the flexibility to respond to opportunities for new initiatives.

Therefore, you may need to pass up certain bids to keep resource allocations flexible. These may even be requirements that you have bid on successfully in the past. This is not an easy decision. Diversification is important and many small clients are preferable to one large client. This is another reason for establishing well thought out bid/no bid checklists or matrixes.

What Is Bid/No Bid Decision Making?

"There is no problem, however complex, that can't be solved by a lack of decision." - unknown

Bid/No Bid Decision Making is risk management through the assessment of the probability of success in submitting a proposal upon receipt of an RFP. This probability can be measured through quantitative or qualitative methodology, or both combined.

Bid/No Bid analysis used correctly is the fastest and easiest way to ensure that you don't waste your time and that you bid only on good opportunities. Why should you bid when the percentage odds of winning are non-existent or near zero per cent? Buying a lottery ticket will give you better odds on winning.

Bid/No Bid analysis is a critical taskl for most firms that prepare competitive proposals. It should be approached in a logical, structured manner. Depending on the size and needs of the firm, the analysis can be very straightforward or very complex. The goal in all cases is the same – assessing the bid and deciding whether to respond or not to respond, using logic as opposed to instinct or hunches.

Bid/No Bid Decision Making
The First Step

Why Do Bid/No Bid Decision Making?

The Firm:

There is considerable pressure within a firm to bid on every opportunity. No one wants to pass up an opportunity to increase business and profitability. This includes sales people, executives new to the firm who want to make a name for themselves, and even the experienced executives who should know that you need to focus your efforts.

Firms monitor different projects that are being developed with the "certain" knowledge that they are going to bid on it, since they know what is wanted.

Conversely, there are new bid opportunities posted daily which may appear to be a close match (or even an almost perfect match). Firms often start preparing proposals for these opportunities without doing any analysis to determine if they should bid.

Decisions on bidding or not bidding are critical to the success of most firms. Resources are limited and each bid incurs an opportunity cost. Bidding on everything occupies important resources that could be better utilized on other activities. This waste of resources can result in the firm continually losing bids, even bids that they should have won. Resources that should have been dedicated to a billable and profitable activity are wasted on a non-billable activity.

Unfortunately, without a measuring system, management tends to be overly optimist and frequently overestimates the chances of their winning proposals.

A Bid/No Bid Analysis is the fastest, easiest, lowest cost way to avoid the trap of bidding unnecessarily. Bidding for the sake of bidding is pointless. No successful firm has the resources to dedicate to the pursuit of everything. It is important to make an informed Bid/No Bid decision when deciding if you are going to respond to an RFP.

There is an Opportunity Cost with random or unfocused bidding as firms have limited resources – resources which could be allocated to more productive activities. Bid/No Bid Analysis is a guide to help focus your attention on opportunities that have a high probability of success. You avoid making random costly decisions to bid on long shots. By limiting the bidding to "good" opportunities, your success ratio will improve.

Focus on the right opportunities. Preparing a proposal is costly. With limited resources, firms can't afford to bid on every request. Successful firms focus on the profitable opportunities and ignore the unprofitable ones.

Staff:

What management often fails to recognize are the negative impacts on the people when a proposal is lost. It is far more than just the lost time, effort and cost. Losing a bid is at a minimum frustrating. Continually losing bids is demoralizing and easily becomes a self-fulfilling prophesy. Executives, staff, partners, associates and sub-contractors start to question the viability of the organization. No one likes to spend a considerable amount of time in non productive work.

The more bids the firm loses, the more people start to question the bidding, such as:
"Why did we lose?"
"What is lacking in the firm?" "
"Should we stop bidding on RFPs?"
"What is wrong with the firm?"
"Is there something that I don't know about?"

Bid/No Bid Decision Making
The First Step

Over time, this can result in the best employees leaving the firm for what they perceive as better opportunities. Everyone loses when this happens. Potential clients may also perceive your reputation as negative and look less favourably on your firm.

The impact is even worse on those who prepared the bids. They have often worked considerable overtime, sacrificing family time and working over weekends. These employees start questioning themselves and their abilities. They also are more likely to blame others, which can have a widespread demoralizing affect.

"What did I do wrong?"
"Why did I bother working all weekend and miss family events?"
"I did a great job, but Fred screwed it up again. Why don't they do something about him?"
"I worked hard. Why don't others pull their own weight?"
"Is it fair that I have to work on a losing team?
"Why did we bother bidding? We know that we always lose."
"Next time, I'm not going to work as hard. Let others do their share."
"Management doesn't care. They didn't give me the help necessary. Why should I care?"
"What a waste of time!"

When you expect to lose, you lose. People perform their best on a winning team, not on a losing team.

Over time, unsuccessful bidding will have a negative impact on staff morale, throughout the firm and in the market place. Lowered motivation equals lowered performance. Staff will no longer produce high-quality proposals.

High quality proposals require extra effort. Why should staff devote extra effort if they perceive that there is no difference in the results? The firm still fails. The long term trend of losing proposals will continue.

On the flip side of the coin, winning energizes everyone – staff, executives, partners, associates and sub-contractors. Everyone who worked hard and sacrificed their personal time feels rewarded knowing that their hard work paid off. Morale rises when people believe that the firm is a "winner". An important fringe benefit is that more contracts mean more work and more job security.

How Do You Make a Bid/No Bid Decision?

There are a number of different approaches to making the Bid/No Bid decision. It is a process with elements that are defined by your firm's capabilities, the expertise of your staff, subcontractors and contract employees, availability of personnel, risk, and financial considerations such as affordability and cash flow.

Bid/No Bid Checklist

No matter how minor or major the proposal, for the majority of firms there is a need for a checklist. Each checklist becomes a template unique to each firm.   It lists all the major items of importance to your firm that are involved in making the Bid/No Bid decision.

While more detail will shortly be provided, a simple question at the top of most checklists is, "Are we qualified to do the job?" There is no point in proceeding further if the answer is "No".

The checklist is straightforward. You simply create a checkmark to the right for each item that is favourable. If you are not certain, then you leave it blank. Place an "X" in every spot that is negative.

If you place an "X" on the first question, "Are we qualified to do the job?" then stop. There is no need to go further.

Bid/No Bid Decision Making
The First Step

Assuming that you place a checkmark on the first question or left it blank, you proceed onward and complete the checklist.

There is no addition or further calculation necessary. Once completed, look over the checklist. It is a guide to organize your thought process and help you decide if you should proceed with a proposal.

A sample Checklist is demonstrated in the following pages.

For ease of assessment, the checklist has been divided into different categories: The Market, The Customer, The Bid, and Our Firm. You may decide to have different categories. For example, there could be a category on Evaluation with questions on Mandatory Criteria, Rated Criteria and Certifications.

 Please keep in mind that the questions shown are for illustration purposes only. You must decide the questions that are valid for your firm.

Bid/No Bid Decision Checklist

Are we qualified to do the job?	

The Customer:

1. Do we know the customer?	
2. Does the customer know us?	
3. Will the evaluators favour our firm?	
4. Do we know who is ultimately going to OK the recommended bid?	
5. Do we know what they want?	

The Market:

6. Do we know the business the customer is in?	
7. Are we known in the business?	
8. Is this our core business?	
9. Do we know how many competitors are bidding, and who they are?	
10. Would winning the bid present future opportunities for other work?	
11. Would winning the bid present future difficulties in performing work for existing clients?	

Bid/No Bid Decision Making
The First Step

The Bid:

12. Do we have enough time to get our proposal ready?	
13. Is the project approved and funded by the client?	
14. Does the requirement have a high risk of project failure?	
15. Is the Bid complex (as opposed to easy to understand)?	
16. Are the evaluation criteria fair and reasonable?	
17. Are there difficulties with the Statement of Work or Requirements?	

Our Firm:

18. Do we have the resources to do the proposal?	
19. Can we accept the contract Terms and Conditions?	
20. Can we manage the cash flow situation that would result	

9. The Proposal Team

Whether your Proposal Team is a Small Team or a Large Team the responsibilities of the Team remain the same. The difference is in the size of the Team that is preparing the proposal.

With a Small Team the responsibilities and duties will be divided amongst the members in a pragmatic manner depending on workload, other commitments, expertise, and position in the firm. The Project Manager may, for example, be the Sales Manager since proposal writing can be considered a sales function.

Should you be in a position of having a Small Team, refer to the responsibilities contained in preparing a proposal for a Large Team. These can be used in structuring and determining the duties of your Small Team.

The Small Team

Most firms only have two or three people who work on the task of preparing proposals. In these cases a common costly mistake is not to have a dedicated resource, - an individual with the duty (and highest level backing) to get the proposal prepared on time. Often, critical delays occur as the proposal sits on a desk because the person is working on other priorities and doesn't have the time or direction that they are to focus on the RFP.

For larger bids, it is absolutely essential to form a team with clear lines of responsibility and accountability. Normally, the RFP response is broken down into sections with the roles and responsibilities of each person, and the deadlines, determined. While most people are technical-oriented or skilled with regard to the subject matter, it is important to have the staff responsible for presentation, layout, graphics and final production at the meeting. It is also important to have, in attendance, the people who are not helping write the proposal but are responsible for the quality control of the proposal (the Red Team). Although often overlooked, a critical group the financial people who will cost the proposal – must attend as well.

The Large Team

In large organizations, roles and responsibilities are divided among a large team. Some of the described positions may not be required due to the complexity, size and structure of the bid. Some of the positions may be combined with one person having more than one role depending on the size of the bidding organization.

The positions below have been listed in categories. The functions and positions described under a category are often combined.

A. Proposal Coordination/Management

Proposal Manager:

This individual has the responsibility and accountability for ensuring that the proposal is produced. The Proposal Manager will direct all the other members of the Proposal Team and ensure that the process is moving smoothly and within time limits. Although the Proposal Team will have a discussion and agreement as to the preparation timelines, this individual is responsible for ensuring that they are realistic and achievable. Should additional resources be required, including specialized expertise, the Proposal Manager is responsible for obtaining them, either from existing internal resources or externally.

The Proposal Manager may or may not be involved in the costing of the proposal. However, the Proposal Manager ensures that all elements of the proposal are costed and that the Costing

Team is aware of all proposed changes to the proposal.

Proposal Coordinator:

This person reports directly to the Proposal Manager and assists the Proposal Manager. The Proposal Coordinator is responsible for monitoring the administration of proposal processes. This includes any reports, changes to the proposal, ensuring deadlines are met and that timelines are respected by all Proposal Team members. The Proposal Coordinator also prepares and provides on-going management status reports regarding the progress of the proposal writing.

B. Specializations

Section Coordinators:

The Section Coordinator normally reports to the Proposal Manager.

Typically, proposals contain sections that have to be addressed separately. For example, the need to demonstrate that you understand the work that is to be done is a separate section from explaining your previous experience doing this type of work. In larger companies, these sections are the responsibility of different individuals.

It is important to note that the sections provided in the RFP, which need to be addressed, may or may not match the breakdown that a firm uses. Good judgment needs to be exercised as to whether to use the firm's breakdown regarding sections or to rigidly apply the RFP breakdown.

The breakdown for preparation of the proposal has to be what makes it easier for the firm to respond. This may mean specific elements of different RFP sections are assigned to one Section

Coordinator, due to the structure of the firm.

The Section Coordinators report to the Proposal Manager who oversees their activities. The Coordinators are accountable for meeting their deadlines while conforming (to the extent possible) to the proposal. Although they may or may not be involved in the writing, they are accountable for the illustrations, the supporting documents, and for ensuring their section is well written and accurate.

They may have to link with other Section Coordinators to ensure that they are providing complete and up-to-date information. One of the worst possible scenarios is the discovery that there is contradictory information between the proposal sections that are prepared due to a simple failure to check that the information and language used was accurate and consistent throughout the proposal.

Specialized Expertise:

These individuals provide specialized expertise such as IT or in-depth knowledge of a particular area of specialization that supports the development of the approach to be used in providing the service.

Very few firms have all the expertise needed in-house. When an RFP arrives, their own experts may be fully employed working for existing clients. Therefore, sub-contractors who have a specialized expertise are used to fill gaps. These need to be managed carefully as they may have no existing obligation to the firm.

Writer:

These individuals write text and provide illustrations for various sections of the proposal. Normally, they report to the Section Coordinator that they work with. Therefore, each writer produces a customized section. They incorporate strategies, CVs, previous experience, etc. and ensure that all elements requested in the RFP are covered. They usually start working when the Section Coordinator receives his/her instructions and they continue working on the proposal through rewrites, amendments, additions and deletions until the final proposal is drafted.

C. Legal and Contracting Advice

Legal Counsel may or may not be needed in developing the proposal. Large, complex proposals normally have legal counsel review the RFP for contractual matters, clauses and omissions that may not be acceptable to the firm. The Counsel may also participate in strategy development to ensure that the proposal is compliant with RFP clauses.

Furthermore, when employed, Legal Counsel reviews the proposal for compliance. In addition, Legal Counsel will prepare the required forms, clauses, representations and certifications for the proposal.

Review of the proposal for legal compliance is not a Red Team function. It is very different. Legal Counsel is reviewing to ensure that legalities are observed and legal problems are addressed. The legal review may be limited to certain sections.

On the other hand, the Red Team review is much broader. It starts with the assumption that the response is legal and is reviewing the proposal for completeness of information and demonstration of ability to perform the functions.

D. Costing:

Costing often appears to be straightforward. There may be existing price lists for the service or goods involved. With a competitive RFP, costing becomes more complex. If you stay with existing rates, you may not win the bid. If you lower the rates too much, you will end up losing money. Someone has to examine all this.

Depending on the complexity, a firm may use an Estimator who is familiar with financial elements of the service or a Cost Analyst who can analyze the complete financial structure of the bid.

This person is responsible for ensuring that all elements of the proposal have been costed. They also have the over-riding responsibility for ensuring that the costing is competitive. This may mean developing a costing strategy for their firm.

Usually they are involved in, but not responsible for, estimating the level of effort (time) and materials necessary to fulfill the contract. However, they are responsible for the costing of the specialized resources (per diems) that will provide the services. They are also responsible for determining the overhead and profit associated with the contract. While these are their responsibilities, often it is the organization management such as the Chief Executive Officer (CEO), Chief Financial Officer (CFO), a Vice President or the Sales Manager who is accountable for the decision on which pricing to use.

E. Layout:

Production Manager:

This individual supervises and coordinates all the production staff including the graphic artist, the desktop publishing expert, layout specialist and final editors. Each RFP usually specifies the number of copies of the proposal to be submitted and if any electronic files are to accompany the copies. Normally, the financial proposal is required to be submitted in a separate document from the technical proposal.

The Production Manager is responsible for correct assembly of all documentation necessary to produce the final proposal. In addition, the Production Manager will work with the Proposal Manager to ensure that the final product is compliant to the RFP.

Graphics/Artwork

This individual provides the illustrations for the proposal. Depending on the organizational structure of the firm, The Graphic Artist may have to work with all the individual section managers to design the presentation of each of their sections. As part of the layout team, the Graphic Artist is responsible for ensuring that there is a visual consistency throughout the proposal and that all graphics are clear and easy to understand.

Desktop Publishing/Layout

In many firms, the Desktop Publishing and Layout functions are combined with the Graphics/Artwork function. As a specialty the individual responsible ensures that the keyboarding uses the same fonts, the layout has the same overall look including indentation, highlighting and titling of sections. An additional responsibility for this individual is to ensure that graphics are placed appropriately and with the correct text. Graphs and illustrations should be near the text that they are linked to.

Editor

The Editor is responsible for ensuring consistency throughout the proposal document. The same style, grammar and technical terms must be used throughout the proposal. Trade jargon is best to be avoided or explained.

The Editor also ensures that re-writes are done to clarify and simplify text.

F. Review Team (Red Team)

The Red Team is responsible for quality control. This function

How to Respond to a RFP
Understanding the Bid and Proposal Process

will be discussed in considerable detail in the next chapter

10. The Red Team

The proposal and bid review function is commonly called "the Red Team". The Red Team is a critical quality control and review component of proposal preparation. It provides an objective viewpoint and a mechanism for improving the quality of the proposal. Done properly, it provides proposal validation and improvements.

This is the task that ensures the proposal meets the requirement of the RFP. Its task is to improve the quality of the proposal and increase the odds of success. Through its analysis of the proposal, it can make the difference between winning and losing.

The Red Team is normally tasked with evaluating and recommending improvement fixes and/or evaluating and scoring the proposal according to the RFP evaluation criteria.

This reviewing function provides an objective viewpoint to both the RFP and the proposal. Preparing a proposal is time consuming. Every RFP item must be checked and double checked. Failing to meet even one item may disqualify your firm from the bidding. Multimillion dollar bids have been lost by small oversights.

It is worth restating the axiom, "You cannot review your own work." The Red Team, through a detailed analysis, will create improvements and eliminate oversights. An oversight can be small but critical, such as forgetting to include a one page document that is a mandatory requirement.

The Red Team accomplishes its tasks by verifying written drafts against the RFP for compliance. Depending on the structure of the Proposal Team, these drafts may be of different sections. Therefore it also compares drafts of the different sections against each other to eliminate contradictions. On the other hand, it will review consecutive drafts of the same sections to ensure clarity and accuracy. Regardless, all final drafts must be verified against the RFP evaluation criteria.

The Red Team normally has at least the following main tasks assigned to it:

- To review the RFP completely and in depth for errors, oversights, contradictions.
- To perform an ongoing review of the answers to questions submitted about the RFP and any amendments issued to the RFP.
- To identify points that need clarification during the bidding process and detail questions that should be asked of the client.
- To provide, during proposal preparation, quality control for oversights and errors/contradictions in information prepared.
- To recommend improvements in proposals of all elements, including content and presentation of information, and to ensure that the proposal is complete.
- To evaluate the proposal as it is prepared against the RFP evaluation criteria. This is not a scoring of the evaluation but it does include completeness, proof reading and clarity of information presented.
- To validate that the final proposal is compliant with the RFP

An important, often overlooked, element of the review by the Red Team is that the Red Team performs an ongoing evaluation of the bid document (RFP) as well as the drafts. This can, and does, result in more questions regarding the RFP that need clarification or changes. The Red Team is also responsible for ensuring new answers to questions do not conflict with draft responses already prepared and, equally important, answers to questions do not conflict with earlier answers or the written RFP.

Through a dedicated Red Team, as already stated, the odds of success are greatly increased. In fact, for most firms that hire outside expertise in proposal preparation, it is the Red Team function that is contracted first. The reason is simple but powerful. It almost goes without saying that Red Team members who are "outsiders" will be more objective than a Red Team composed of employees of the firm.

Organizing the Red Team

Most bids are of a size that they require a Red Team consisting of only one person who reviews both the RFP and the proposal. They may possibly have a back-up person. However, large multi-volume detailed proposals may require more than one person.

The following is written for situations where there are two or more people on the Red Team. However the points being made are still valid in the case of a single person Red Team.

The first item of business is to appoint a Red Team Leader. This is the person who will provide and/or direct activities and be responsible for coordinating the results.

The Red Team leader must be respected. In other words the organization must believe that the Red Team will make a difference. The leader directs the efforts of any other members and participates in the review process.

The leader is an extension of the Red Team concept. The leader is not involved in content development but is responsible for collecting and coordinating Red Team comments.

The next item of business is to have a Red Team orientation session. It is vital that all Red Team members understand the same goals and use the same procedures. Each Red Team Member normally reviews only the sections of the proposal that the Red Team leader has assigned.

The Red Team, whether one person or more, reviews for compliance, clarity, clarifications, the response to the evaluation criteria, organization and layout and completeness of information,

Three cautions need to be added. First, you should avoid using senior executives of your firm as a reviewer. Without meaning to, they will influence the development and content of the proposal. They are managers and will read the proposal, unavoidably, from a manager's viewpoint. The proposal has to be written from the viewpoint of the client.

Second, it may be desirable to have a technical review of the proposal to improve, and to validate technical content for completeness. This is parallel to and separate from the Red Team function. It is not considered a Red Team function.

Third, if there is a need for legal examination, the Legal Review proceeds under the auspices of the Proposal Manager. This is not considered a Red Team Function.

Red Team Attitude

It is important to ensure that no one feels threatened by the Red Team. Some people resent having their work checked, feeling that they are being criticized. The Red Team is not about finding problems with staff. It is about preventing problems with the proposal. The Red Team will provide suggestions for improvements and point out oversights.

Everyone has to realize that the Red Team is about winning and improving the proposal. The Red Team is "part of the solution, not part of the problem."

Red Team Reviews

The first review is of the RFP and all amendments to ensure that it is complete and there is a clear understanding of how to respond.

The second and by far the most complicated and time consuming review, is the review of the proposal. There are usually many drafts that may be created for different sections. It is helpful to have a guide or checklist of these drafts to ensure that this review is complete. This helps prevent misunderstandings regarding the responsibilities of the Red Team.

While the following questions are offered as a helpful guide, they may not address the needs of every firm. As you read the list, take note of the questions being asked. The Red Team is doing more than a simple check. For example, it is examining the proposal for content improvement, (Q5, Q11) and presentation (Q12).

The Red Team is not normally involved in pricing the solution. However, the Red Team may offer suggestions regarding the Basis of Payment and method of evaluation. Often there are different approaches that can be suggested which reduce various risks, such as exchange rate fluctuations.

Red Team Review

Question	Yes/No
Is the draft proposal solution feasible and does it work?	
Does the draft proposal meet all the elements of the evaluation criteria?	
Have all the benefits of the services been pointed out?	
Do all elements of the Proposal address all elements of the RFP? This includes mandatory and evaluated requirements, certifications, warranties, resumes, insurance, etc.	
Is there anything missing that needs to be added?	
Is there anything that should be deleted for better clarity?	
Is the language used positive and informative – as opposed to negative and condescending?	
Are there contradictions between various sections within the draft? In most cases, the sections are produced by different people and consistency can become a problem.	
Is the terminology used by different drafters consistent?	
Are there changes and corrections that need to be done?	
Are there suggestions that can be made to improve the quality of the proposal?	
Are the graphics, illustrations or charts in the correct location and easily understood?	

Red Team Failures

A Red Team review should be done on every proposal. This review, done by people other than those who wrote the proposal, can make the difference between a win or a loss.

In spite of all efforts, there are times when the Red Team concept does not work. This is most common when a firm does all the work in-house rather than hire a professional.

There are a variety of reasons for this failure but all have a common element. It is the internal structure or dynamics, not the value of a review function that may cause the failure of a Red Team. However, if you understand what has caused this problem, you can find a solution for it.

Some major reasons for Red Team failure are:

Communication

- The participants are not clearly told what to expect from a Red Team.
- The Red Team's advice is resented and not followed.
- It is not clear that the Proposal Manager is in charge of the proposal but not in charge of the Red Team.
- The Red Team members are also employees of the firm with other conflicting duties and priorities.
- There is no understood relationship between the Red Team's comments and the evaluation criteria.
- Red Team comments are only suggestions. Proposal writers take them as orders instead of treating them as recommendations.
- It is not understood that proposal writers have the "decision authority" over content.

How to Respond to a RFP
Understanding the Bid and Proposal Process

Review

- The Red Team wants to change the structure or outline of the proposal. This is not a Red Team decision.
- The Red Team does not explain the reason for their recommendations. Changes must be explained.
- Comments are made in different formats by different reviewers
- The Red Team looks at the proposal from the viewpoint of the bidder instead of the viewpoint of the customer.
- Red Team comments fail to recognize that there may be a page limitation incorporated into the RFP.
- The Red Team contradicts the RFP.
- Red Team members make general comments without explaining action required.
- The Red Team doesn't analyze or offer any useful advice or help.

Responsibilities

- The Red Team members are not given direction.
- The Red Team members do not understand the Red Team concept.
- The Red Team members do not understand the evaluation function.
- The Red Team members do not read the RFP.
- The Red Team identify problems but do NOT identify solutions.
- The Red Team only does proofreading, not analysis.
- The Red Team expects to see the document again after changes are made, but do not.

Structure

- The same people who write the proposal are on the Red

Team.
- People are assigned to the Red Team who don't want to be there.
- Some people are on the Red Team because they want the prestige or to just read the document but are not able to provide meaningful advice.

Scheduling

- Red Team does not start evaluating RFP immediately on receipt of it by the firm
- Red Team proposal evaluation is commenced too late and there is not enough time to evaluate and incorporate recommendations. If the proposal is fatally flawed, there is no time to correct the problem.

Goals

- The Red Team points out deficiencies in the bid without offering useful advice or suggestions for improvement
- Everyone has a different definition of what a "Red Team" is.
- Goals for the Red Team are not defined and understood.

Fixing the Red Team

Should there be a problem, the methodology to fix the Red Team is basic management problem solving. The same methods that you would use in restructuring an organization are used for the Red Team.

Meeting

Have an emergency meeting of everyone involved in proposal preparation to discuss the situation. The reason for the emergency is basic. The clock is ticking and there is no time to waste if the proposal is going to be written and submitted.

Misunderstandings are often easy to solve if you can have people talk to each other. Allow at least an hour. Discuss the roles and responsibilities and expectations of all parties. This understanding should have been created at the initial proposal meeting prior to work starting on the response. However, a further discussion of the roles and responsibilities can be used to solve the problem.

Set your goals

Ensure the Red Team and Proposal Team understand what is expected of them. The Proposal Team is responsible for decisions on technical content, enhancements, proposal writing including layout and graphics. The Red Team is responsible for recommendations – improvements, preventing omissions, ensuring compliance, evaluation mapping.

Training

The Red Team is a critical function and must have a knowledgeable and capable leader. Red Team members often do not know what is expected of them. Sometimes they were ordered by management to join the Red team but not given any guidance or training.

The training to Red Team members can be provided by the Red Team Leader. However, being a member of a Red Team is not a job for a new employee. It requires skilled, knowledgeable employees who have dealt with RFPs before. Many firms choose to contract with an expert for the Red Team function. This avoids the Red Team becoming the "weakest link" in the bid process.

Time Commitments

This is the most common problem that needs solving. Problems with time usually reflect a misunderstanding of need for this commitment or a conflict with other on-going work that the team members have. Red Team members must be made aware that they must dedicate a considerable amount of time to Red Team Priorities.

For the RFP, there is the time needed to do an initial review of the RFP, to prepare questions and to carry out the ongoing review of amendments. For the Proposal, there is the time needed to review all drafts, to verify compliance against the RFP and to ensure consistency of information in proposal development.

When you consider the time taken for all the above functions, it is a minimum of 35 hours to respond to even a basic RFP. This time is no longer available for regular or other responsibilities and everyone should be clearly aware of this.

When there is a conflict with existing work, all levels of management has to fully commit that the Red Team work is the number one priority. Unless that is made clear, and enforced, the Red Team will continue to operate inefficiently and the quality of the proposal will suffer.

Positive Attitude

Proposal team members have to understand that the Red Team is not searching for problems. The Red Team is a quality control function. It focuses on improving the proposal, not criticizing the author(s) of the draft section(s).

The goal is to have zero errors. A good Red Team helps and offers suggestions and improvements. Improvements equate to success. Success equates to winning. The Red Team is there to help the firm and the staff to achieve their goal of developing a high quality proposal and winning the bid.

How to Respond to a RFP
Understanding the Bid and Proposal Process

11. A Team of One

Smaller firms have limited resources. As a consequence, they often make the mistake of having just one person prepare a proposal in response to an RFP. This means that the writer is now the editor. The Proposal Manager is the Proposal Team and, at the same time, the Red Team.

The Red Team

Combining the two roles is a difficult task. There is no backup or error checking that can be done. If you make a mistake it is usually fatal.

What do you do when there is no separate Red Team? As a "Team of One" from your viewpoint, the Red Team function has been narrowed and is more limited. It is no longer a review function for the proposal.

The Red Team role focuses on an analysis of the RFP and any subsequent amendments in-depth for errors, oversights and contradictions. This includes identifying points that need clarification.

In one respect the role expands. Instead of just identifying questions that should be asked with respect to the RFP, the Red Team function now includes asking those questions. Other firms will be asking questions at the same time. Any answers to questions on the RFP must be verified for completeness, oversights and contradictions.

The Proposal Team

When you are a "Team of One", it is usually more difficult to write the proposal well than to know what to write. You are tasked, not only with ensuring the proposal meets the evaluation criteria of the RFP, but also with ensuring that a quality proposal is produced.

How can you edit your own work? How can you criticize your own work? Since it is what you said, it must be right. Although the fact that you are both reviewer and writer is not the best situation, there is a way to cope.

Writing the Proposal

Try and be concise in what you write. When writing a speech with limited time duration, I have spent much of the time trying to consolidate words and thoughts to eliminate unnecessary words. The same philosophy applies to proposal writing. Don't use a phrase when a word will do. Use just one idea per sentence. Short meaningful sentences are better than sentences that go on and on and on.....

Don't write as if you are uninterested and not involved. In other words, don't write using passive words, use active words. You don't want to "consider a course of action"; you want to "implement an approach to resolve the problem".

Be careful using words with double meanings. For example, bi-monthly can mean twice a month or every two months. The same applies to bi-weekly. Be careful not to create confusion.

Guard against making typing mistakes that the spell checker will not catch. These are the ones that you make when you type. Each of us has different words that can cause errors. For example, I often type "not" when I mean "now". The meaning of the sentence is completely different when you type, "It is now time to do..." instead of, "It is not time to do..." The other error that I often make is between "rational" and "rationale". The second is not a serious as the first error.

A Team of One

Step 1:

Start by writing any section of the proposal. Remember that it is a draft. You don't have to worry about being complete. The important thing is to get your thoughts down in writing. Check it with spell check and then put it aside. Go work on another section of the proposal.

I have done this many times with major success. The longer that you can leave it aside, the better are the odds that you will rewrite the proposal or the section of the proposal that you were working on. We are not talking weeks or months but hours or a couple of days. This is a response to an RFP so you don't have unlimited time.

Step 2:

Next, re-open the draft section and read it carefully. Rewrite anything that seems to need improvement, spell check it, close it. Once again go work on another section.

Step 3:

Repeat as necessary (if you have time) until you are confident that the draft sections are well-written and RFP compliant.

Step 4:

After writing, go back and check your math. In the first course that I gave on basic proposal writing, I forgot to check the math. I was illustrating the calculations for determining the winner of a contract and had stated which firm won the contract. One of the attendees pointed out that I had made a simple calculation error. Once this error was corrected, a different firm became the winner. This is a prime example of how difficult it is to check your own work.

How to Respond to a RFP
Understanding the Bid and Proposal Process

Step 5:

As you write the proposal, be sure to verify that it conforms to the RFP. The final step is to do a full evaluation of the finished proposal against the RFP. Ensure that the information is complete, all RFP evaluation criteria have been met and the proposal is clear and well organized.

12. Reviewing Bid Documents

It is well to keep in mind that the term, RFP, throughout this book is used in its generic context, unless otherwise stated.

An RFP is a formal document describing the project, how the contractor should respond and how proposals will be reviewed. It includes contact information for the contractors bidding the project. The following overview will be discussed in more depth later on.

It is critical that the RFP be immediately analyzed. Businesses are often focused on day to day issues and ignore this need, to their detriment. Often there are critical questions that need to be answered quickly.

There is a logical order in reviewing the RFP.

First, start with the Statement of Work. It may also be called the Requirements Definition or Description of Goods. In any case, it is the part of the RFP that describes the work or service that is to be provided. Before spending more time on the RFP, you want and need to know if you have the expertise or capability to respond.

Second, read the evaluation criteria. Find out if there are restrictions that would preclude you from bidding. In the event you do not meet the criteria, ask yourself if the RFP evaluation criteria are fair and if they were changed would this enable you to bid.

Third, and finally, read the rest of the document. This will complete your understanding of the RFP. Following the review in the order described will maximize your productive time.

Once you have decided to bid, you can commence analyzing the complete document in depth. Read the RFP, identifying and making notes on items that appear to need further clarification or which are not written clearly.

Review all the elements focusing on the evaluation criteria. Again make notes on items that appear to need further clarification or revision. It is careful attention to the evaluation criteria section that will determine if you will succeed.

Plan your response. Create a timeline for preparing the proposal, allowing time for corrections and review. List all the elements that need to be completed.

Assemble your response team and discuss all the tasks and elements, who will do each of them and when they need to be completed by. Seek input from the response team and determine if there are further questions that need to be asked.

Pay close attention to the instructions and make sure that you fully understand them. While you can telephone the procurement officer for general clarifications, don't be surprised if the purchasing officer advises you to submit your questions in writing by the method of your choice - letter, fax or e-mail.

An important thought that needs to be kept in mind is that not all questions should be asked. While poor writing or oversights can be corrected, it may be an advantage to leave them intact.

13. Decoding the RFP

Look upon the RFP as a document written in code. It is your job to decode it. The purpose of this "decoding' is to be certain that the proposal will respond to each and every element of the RFP. It is usually necessary to translate the RFP into simple language that is understandable to you to enable you to prepare a proposal.

This will help to ensure that there are no gaps in the information received. In order to be considered you must be compliant with all RFP instructions and the evaluation criteria. Reponses must reflect the weighting (if known) of the evaluation criteria.

Did you understand the bidding instructions? Read them carefully. This is an area that creates confusion as language can, at times, be read in different ways with different meanings. Make sure you fully understand the instructions. Once you understand the importance of what is written and what you have to complete, you can start a full review and analysis of the RFP.

Read the RFP scope of work in depth first. Does it contain terminology that is proprietary to another firm? Both Kleenex and Scotch Tape are examples of terms that have become generic in normal conversation. However, in an RFP you will see the products more correctly referred to using technical terms such as paper tissue or tape. In this way competitor brands to Kleenex or Scotch Tape can be considered.

In the computer industry, technology has not produced the same high degree of standardization. The RFP may contain a trade name, inadvertently, that would prohibit some bidders including you. If this is the case, prepare and send a question regarding such content in the RFP. Follow up to see if the description is amended.

As you read, make a list of everything that you notice that is unclear in the RFP with a reference as to where you noticed it. You may find the answers to some items on the list as you continue reading. If so, you can check off your earlier observation. Before you do so, write a cross reference on the RFP so that you don't have to search for the answer again.

Next, create an internal project plan to determine how you will address the answers to the remaining questions.

Most RFPs consist of both mandatory and evaluation criteria.

Mandatory Requirements

There are three critical words that will appear throughout the RFP: 'Will', 'Shall' and 'Must'.

MUST:

These are obligatory requirements which you must address in your proposal. They fall into two categories – obvious and less obvious. "Obvious" is the list of mandatory requirements which are provided. "Less obvious" are the mandatory requirements that are not identified in a separate section but which still exist.

WILL/SHALL:

Every "will" or "shall" in the RFP is a requirement that you will be obligated to fulfill should you win the contract. Often they will be included in the mandatory list through a blanket statement such as: The bidder certifies that it accepts all the terms and conditions contained herein".

A second possibility is that the rated evaluation criteria required the bidder to demonstrate compliance by meeting a minimum score.

The third possibility is that you were not requested to respond to the statement at all. In this case, it is a given that the winning firm will be contractually obligated to fulfill these requirements.

A. Hidden Mandatory Criteria:

Although it is not commonly understood, there are actually two types of mandatory criteria. The first, and well known, is the mandatory criteria that are listed in the same section as the rated evaluation criteria. The second, less known and often overlooked, are the Hidden Mandatory requirements.

These appear throughout the RFP in different sections.

By doing this, the client is defining the rules of the competitive bid process. These rules are normally not negotiable. You may not have to address these Hidden Mandatory requirements in your written proposal but, should you win, they will become part of the contract.

Before analyzing the listed mandatory and point rated criteria, go through the RFP line by line. Highlight every 'will', 'shall' or 'must' that you encounter.

When you find a Hidden Mandatory that, in your opinion, presents a problem the solution is to write a Question regarding the RFP, requesting that the criteria be amended.

This early review will prevent later problems.

B. Listed Mandatory Criteria:

In order for your bid to be evaluated and considered responsive, it is critical to meet all the listed mandatory criteria. The listed Mandatory requirements can be determined quickly by asking yourself, "Can I meet this?" If you cannot answer yes, then you know not to bid.

These criteria are supposed to be evaluated objectively and on a simple pass/fail basis. Only proposals that meet all the mandatory criteria are considered to have been responsive.

Since only responsive proposals receive a further evaluation, write carefully and address every mandatory requirement carefully and completely.

As part of the review exercise, ask yourself:

- Are these criteria fair?
- Are there criteria that are not necessary?
- Are the criteria clear or do they need judgment?
- Are any of the criteria biased in favour of one or more specific firms?

Evaluation (Point Rated) Criteria

Once it has been determined that a proposal has met the mandatory criteria, it is then evaluated against the point- rated criteria. This is the area where the majority of work should have been done by the bidder when preparing a competitive proposal.

The mandatory criteria have already covered whether a firm is capable of performing the service or not. In theory, the point rated evaluation criteria are used to evaluate "value" or "quality" factors. This will determine the technical merit of each proposal

A word often used in the evaluation is "demonstrate". In other words – prove it. As the next stage in the evaluation process, these criteria are used to evaluate the ability to do the work over and above the minimum qualifications required (mandatory requirements).

The maximum points that can be achieved for each criterion are normally identified in the RFP. The more completely that you can prove that you can perform the service, the more marks that can be obtained.

The same four questions that were asked for the mandatory criteria apply to the evaluation criteria with two additions.

- Are these criteria fair?
- Are there criteria that are not necessary?
- Are the criteria clear or do they need judgment?
- Are any of the criteria biased in favour of one or more specific firms?
- Is the weighting of the points allocated fair?
- How the points are to be evaluated?

When in doubt, prepare a written question to be sent to the procurement officer. Put it aside. Have someone else read it. Does it ask what you want to ask? Be precise. Just because you want to raise a question, doesn't mean that you should. Not asking may be to your advantage. You may want to discuss this with the Red Team Leader.

Do not wait until responses to questions are received. Start drafting the proposal response immediately in order to maximize the use of time. You can always amend your proposal responses when answers to questions are received

Keep in mind that in order to be judged responsive, a proposal has to achieve a minimum number of points through the rated evaluation. This does not mean that the proposal will win the bid, as more than one firm may have been judged "responsive". Therefore, every point becomes critical. Bids have been won or lost based on one or two points in the rated evaluation.

The result of being judged responsive is that the proposal moves to the next step in the process as defined in the RFP.

How to Respond to a RFP
Understanding the Bid and Proposal Process

14. Problems with RFPs

As you analyze RFPs, you will find many problems within them – problems that need to be corrected if you are to maximize your odds of winning.

- There can be too little or too much detail in an RFP. Many writers of the Statement of Work/Requirement (SOW) micromanage the information. Instead of stating what they want, they end up describing how to do the service in precise terms. Conversely, the SOW could describe only an outcome rather than give important technical details.

- Large RFPs have a problem unique to themselves. Due to their size, they end up having different writers. Contradictions and confusion often result between sections.

- The SOW and Evaluation Criteria can become disorganized. Before issuing the bid, the customer should have had someone thoroughly look over the RFP, but they didn't. The result is more work for you.

- The RFP can, and often does, specify staffing requirements and levels of education/experience that far exceed the actual need. That can make it extremely difficult to create an organization chart and ensure sufficient staffing levels to meet these RFP compliance levels.

- Delivery dates within the RFP can be contradictory.

- There is often no linkage between the requirement and the evaluation criteria. The evaluation might introduce new requirements that are not part of the SOW. For example, the RFP might be for provision of quality control services but the evaluation is based on risk management services.

How to Respond to a RFP
Understanding the Bid and Proposal Process

- In some RFPs (fortunately the minority) the instructions are vague and it is unclear how to organize or present the proposal. In fact, it might not even be clear how the proposal is going to be evaluated.

- From the viewpoint of the bidder, there might be a need for clarification. However the clarification could reduce their competitive edge or place the customer in the position of admitting that they did not know what they were doing.

15. How to Analyze Evaluation Criteria

When writing a good proposal, it is essential to develop a methodology that will ensure that everything is complete and nothing is inadvertently overlooked. An important skill for a proposal writer to develop is the ability to view the rated evaluation criteria of an RFP from the evaluator's viewpoint.

The goal of the evaluator is to bring objectivity (how to evaluate the bid) to subjectivity (the quality of the service to be provided). Evaluators are obligated to follow the evaluation criteria as written. It is therefore important to understand how to read evaluation criteria. Not all evaluators will analyze in depth but you should write your proposal with the assumption that you are going to have the toughest evaluator possible.

The following examples are excerpts from an actual RFP and presented in detail to illustrate how to analyze written criteria. The section numbers used are the numbers as presented in the RFP. It is important to note that as the evaluation criteria becomes longer with more detail, the complexity of the analysis increases.

Example 1: Simple Criteria

The Evaluation Criteria:

Proponents are to describe their corporate vision for the provision of fleet management services over the next five years. This should include a description of:

- *the Proponent's priorities for improving service to customers*

This example is of interest for two reasons. The first point has nothing to do with the actual analysis. The word "proponent" was used instead of "bidder", "firm" or even "resulting contractor". Any of these words or even the use of other words would have be equally acceptable as long as the meaning of the word remains clear. It is not unusual for clients to have their own favourite wording.

The Analysis:

There are three different components addressed in the evaluation criteria as follows:

1) The proponent's priorities
2) for improving service
3) to customers

However, there is only one possible response to the evaluation criteria, "The Proponent's priorities for improving service to customers". None of the three above components gave alternatives to respond to.

Example 2: Some Complexity

The Evaluation Criteria:

(c)…confirmed new services and other services that may be introduced by the Proponent to customers;

The Analysis:

There are two different components addressed in the above evaluation criteria as follows:

1) confirmed new services and other services that may be introduced

2) for improving service to customers.

As a result, there are two possible answers as item 1) contains two different items as follows:

- confirmed new services to the customers
- other services that may be introduced to the customers

Both of these evaluation criteria have to be addressed in the proposal to have a complete response.

Example 3: Confusion or Complexity?

The Evaluation Criteria:

(f) general trends and developments in the automotive industry or regulatory environment that may impact the Province;

The Analysis:

As the complexity increases, the evaluation becomes more difficult to follow. It is again necessary to break it down into its components. This time, a different methodology will be used due to the increased complexity and the need to be certain not to overlook anything.

Repeating the evaluation criteria, indicators of the breakdown necessary are added.
general trends and developments (2 elements)
in the automotive industry or regulatory environment
(2 more elements)
that may impact the Province;

We now discover that we have 2 elements x 2 elements = 4 elements to respond to in our proposal. To repeat, the RFP used "...trends and developments." (2 elements) and "...industry or regulatory..."(2 elements).

The breakdown is as follows with the key words in italics:

- *general trends* in the *automotive* industry that may impact the Province
- *general trends* in the *regulatory* environment that may impact the Province
- *developments* in the *automotive* industry that may impact the Province
- *developments* in the *regulatory* environment that may impact the Province

Note that "general trends"., "developments", "automotive" and "regulatory" all appear twice in different combinations.

Example 4: The Layers of Complexity

The following is the final and most complex example. At this point it is worth noting that evaluation criteria can be even more complex than any of the four examples illustrated. However the methodology presented prevents oversights and errors in completion of proposals.

It is important to be able to follow each and every element in all their variations to ensure nothing is overlooked. It is very likely that the evaluators will not look at the proposal in such depth but you can not be certain.

The Evaluation Criteria:

Proponents are to describe the tools and strategies that they currently employ to assist customers to reduce vehicle greenhouse gas emissions. Proponents should specifically address tools and strategies to:

(a) ensure that individual vehicles are operating at optimal

capacity.

(*b*) *facilitate information exchanges designed to inform fleet managers and manufacturers about operational benefits and challenges associated with this expanding technology;*

The Analysis:

The key is to break the evaluation down into its components, step by step. Repeating the evaluation criteria as was done in Example 3, indicators of the breakdown necessary are added.

"Proponents are to describe the 1) tools and 2) strategies (2 elements) that they currently employ to assist customers to reduce vehicle greenhouse gas emissions. Proponents should specifically address tools and strategies to:

(a) ensure that individual vehicles are operating at optimal capacity.(1 element)

(b) facilitate information exchanges designed to inform 3) fleet managers and 4) manufacturers (2 elements) about 5) operational benefits and 6) challenges (2 elements) associated with this expanding technology;"

The analysis then starts by breaking down the elements in the order that they appear. The first breakdown is *tools* and *strategies* which is just 2 elements to evaluate.

(a) requires that you ensure individual vehicles are operating at optimal efficiency. This is one element so 1 x 2 = 2 elements to evaluate as follows:

- *Tools* to ensure that individual vehicles are operating at optimal efficiency;
- *Strategies* to ensure that individual vehicles are operating at optimal efficiency.

(b) is different. It starts with information exchanges to inform fleet *managers* and *manufacturers*. These are two elements. Next you have to discuss *operational benefits* and *challenges* which are two more elements. Initially the total to analyze appear to be 2 x 2 = 4 elements to evaluate. This is incorrect. You have to work back up to the original introduction which called for a description of *tools* and *strategies*. So what you are faced with is 2 x 2 x 2 = 8 elements.

In other words:

2 (*fleet managers and manufacturers*) x 2 (*operational benefits and challenges*) x 2) (*tools and strategies*) = 8

To avoid oversights and ensure nothing is overlooked, it helps to write it out with a full breakout. Start with the original breakdown of tools and strategies and add in the other elements as follows:

Tools

- The *tools* to facilitate information exchanges designed to inform *fleet managers* about *operational benefits* associated with this expanding technology;
- The *tools* to facilitate information exchanges designed to inform *fleet managers* about *operational challenges* associated with this expanding technology;
- The *tools* to facilitate information exchanges designed to inform *manufacturers* about *operational benefits* associated with this expanding technology
- The *tools* to facilitate information exchanges designed to inform *manufacturers* about *operational challenges* associated with this expanding technology

Strategy

- The *strategy* to facilitate information exchanges designed to inform *fleet managers* about *operational benefits* associated

with this expanding technology;
- The *strategy* to facilitate information exchanges designed to inform *fleet managers* about *operational challenges* associated with this expanding technology;
- The *strategy* to facilitate information exchanges designed to inform *manufacturers* about *operational benefits* associated with this expanding technology.
- The *strategy* to facilitate information exchanges designed to inform *manufacturers* about *operational challenges* associated with this expanding technology.

It is important that you create a checklist, especially when you have conflicting duties. Normally you would not create a breakdown as written above. A brief checklist would be created. For the above, a checklist would be a simple as:

Tools – Fleet Managers – Benefits
Tools – Fleet Managers – Challenges
Tools – Manufacturers – Benefits
Tools – Manufacturers – Challenges
Strategy – Fleet Managers – Benefits
Strategy – Fleet Managers – Challenges
Strategy – Manufacturers – Benefits
Strategy - Manufacturers - Challenges

This checklist is much shorter than the detailed analysis but contains the same information and serves as a guide when writing the proposal.

As a means of verification, you can just count the number of times each element appears on the list. In this case, since they were all linked in twos, all the elements appear four times each :Tools, Strategy, Fleet Managers, Manufacturers, Benefits, Challenges.

The Proposal Response

In the first three examples, no suggested proposal response was offered. In answering the evaluation criteria, you do not need to create a separate paragraph or explanation for each component or element.

They can be blended and your answer could say:

"The tools that will be used to inform both fleet managers and manufacturers of the benefits are..." Note that you have now covered two elements in one sentence.

You could also have said, "The tools that will be used to inform both fleet managers and manufacturers of the benefits and challenges are..." In this way you covered four elements in one sentence. The key is to ensure that no components or elements are missed.

In other words, the response for the elements may be simplified but you must answer all elements to avoid oversights. Also a general rule applies, "when in doubt, write it out." Points are not awarded for brevity. They are awarded for clarity.

Guidance:

Often there is guidance written into the RFP document. Take note of any guidance offered and use it to your advantage.

Example 1:

Proponents with on-line ordering capability should include a demonstration of their system during the Fleet Management Information System presentations to the evaluation committee (see section 23.3).

In this case, you are being referred to another section of the RFP in order to give you more information on what the demonstration is to entail.

Example 2:

Proponents offering Internet marketing and sales tools for vehicle disposal should include an overview of their system during the presentation to the evaluation committee (see section 25.0).

In this case, you are again being referred to another section of the RFP in order to give you more information. You are also being informed that an overview of your system should be included in any forthcoming presentation. Failure to include an overview will result in reduced marks.

16. How "Rated Requirements" are Evaluated

Knowing that you have to ensure all elements are answered is important, but it also helps to have an understanding of how evaluations may be done.

The following examples will give an illustration of two of the more common approaches.

Example 1 – Complex Point Rating

This is an evaluation methodology often used when the evaluators do not have a predetermined answer. Bidders, in their proposals, can add to the information being supplied to gain more marks in the rated evaluation. Take note that this method is essentially based on evaluating each and every element.

The Grid is given to the evaluators and serves as the guide to evaluation. To some degree, subjectivity still exists in this methodology.

This evaluation grid is based on a score of 0 to 10 where 0 is a failure and 10 are full marks. If you follow each score, you can see a progression in the information that is being requested.

Evaluation Grid

Failed - 0 points
- issue/requirement not addressed
- details not provided
- lacked understanding
- approach is totally unclear

How to Respond to a RFP
Understanding the Bid and Proposal Process

Inadequate - 2 points
- requirement is superficially addressed
- insufficient details provided
- key issue/requirement not addressed
- poor level of understanding displayed

Satisfactory - 5 points
- issue/requirement generally addressed
- some details missing
- need for much clarification
- level of understanding is incomplete
- approach to implementation is unclear

Good - 7 points
- most issues/requirements addressed well
- a few details missing
- some additional clarification needed
- displays good level of understanding

Very Good - 8 points
- all issues/requirements addressed well
- provided detailed responses to all elements of the requirement
- demonstrated clear understanding of our needs
- demonstrated that they can meet all requirements and timeframes
- responses are logical and believable
- where applicable, statements of compliance (i.e. guarantee, acknowledgement, undertaking, etc.)

Excellent – 9 points
- all issues/requirements addressed clearly and linked to all other aspects of the RFP
- demonstrated clear understanding of RFP needs and service concepts

- provided job descriptions for each of the people when necessary

Superior – 10 points
in addition to items in Excellent, the following:
- makes us aware of issues which may arise that would negatively impact the service
- provides a clear understanding of government and service limitations, if any, and proposes work around plans
- provides a thorough definition of how the work is performed

The above grid is strictly an example. There are many variations depending on the RFP and the clients involved.

There may be fewer categories: Failed – 0 points, Inadequate – 4 points, Good – 7 points, Excellent – 10 points.

Whether there are fewer or more categories, there is a progression in the weight assigned based on completeness of the information given in the proposal. To illustrate this, take the first item listed on the grid for each rating and list them in table format. A quick glance will show that each proposal is being assessed on completeness of information. The more information supplied, the higher the score that a bidder will receive.

Rating	Commentary
Failed	Issue/requirement not addressed
Inadequate	requirement is superficially addressed
Satisfactory	issue/requirement generally addressed
Good	most issues/requirements addressed well
Very Good	all issues/requirements addressed well
Excellent	all issues/requirements addressed clearly and linked to all other aspects of the RFP
Superior	Items in addition to items in Excellent

The Evaluation:

The above evaluation grid was used to show that every item is being evaluated in the same way. Whether a more complex or less complex grid is used, the goal is to reward proposals that are detailed and which enable the evaluator to understand what is being offered.

The next step is to recognize that every evaluation item has its own weight. For example, let's suppose the RFP had five items to evaluate: Staffing Plan, Delivery, Technical Solutions, Management Plan, and Understanding of the Requirement.

How Rated Requirements are Evaluated

Not all of these items are equally important. Some are more important than others. Therefore, every evaluation item will have its own weight. In the above example we will use the following:

A. Staffing Plan	10 points
B. Delivery	5 points
C. Technical Solutions	20 points
D. Management Plan	10 points
E. Understanding of the Requirement	<u>15 points</u>
Total	60 points

With the total mark given for all five items being 60 and each element being evaluated separately, the following chart shows how the final mark might be determined. The formula used is:

Total marks available x mark received (out of 10) = final total mark for the element.

Examples:
Calculation for A is: 10 x 8/10 = 8.
Calculation for E is: 15 x 9/10 = 13.5

Evaluation Element	Weight	Evaluation Mark (out of 10)	Total
A. Staffing Plan	10	8	8
B. Delivery	5	10	5
C. Technical Solutions	20	7	14
D. Management Plan	10	5	5
E. Understanding of Requirement	15	9	13.5
Totals	**60**		**45.5**

In this case the total mark received by the bidder for their proposal would have been 45.5/60 = 75.8%.

If the qualifying mark had been set at 70%, the firm would be considered responsive (pass) and still be in the running for the contract. .

If the qualifying mark had been set at 80%, the firm would be considered non-responsive and not considered further.

Example 2: Objective Point Rating

Another way that point rated evaluation is approached is to look for objective criteria. A point-rated score based on numbers that can be easily verified. This could be the years of experience for personnel, the number of projects completed or academic qualifications.

This methodology is less prone to error. However, it limits the ability of firms to offer the best solutions in their proposal. On the flip side of the coin, it limits the clients ability to receive the best solution since they predetermined what needed to be offered.

If years of experience are used as an example, the point evaluation may appear as follows:

Years of Experience:
0 years experience = 0 points
1 to 3 years experience = 2 points
4 to 6 years experience = 5 points
6 to 8 years experience = 8 points
More than 8 years experience = 10 points

By its nature, this can (and does on some RFPs) penalize a new person, right out of school, with the exact technical skills required over a person who has been working for years and not kept their knowledge up-to-date.

17. How Price Factors into the Evaluation

Firms who have successfully met the mandatory requirement and the point rated requirements are now assessed on their financial or price quotation. This is usually the final stage in the evaluation process.

At this stage, proposals are now evaluated on a blending of rated requirements (quality) and price. The three most common methods of evaluation will be described along with how each method affects the final outcome of the bidding process.

Every RFP must be examined to determine the evaluation methodology that is being used and the proposal adjusted accordingly. There are a number of different methods of determining price.

Method 1: Lowest Price Per Point:

This is the most common evaluation mechanism. The evaluation is a blending of quality (rated evaluation criteria) with price. The firm assessed with lowest price per point wins the contract.

The following example demonstrates how Lowest Price Per Point works.

In this example, the rated evaluation criteria was set at a 70% threshold. Three firms achieved more than 70%.

Firm A – total points 80
Firm B – total points 71
Firm C – total points 85

A separate price evaluation was held and it was determined that the following total prices were submitted by each firm:

Firm A - $105,000
Firm B - $ 99,000
Firm C - $115,000

The evaluation then proceeds to determine the best value which, in this case, is defined as lowest price per point. The formula is a follows:

Total Price/Total Points = Price per Point.

The evaluation proceeded as follows:

Firm	Total Dollars/Total Points	Price per point
A	$105,000/80	$1,312.50*
B	$ 99,000/71	$1,394.37
C	$115,000/85	$1,352.29

* winning proposal

Although it is not always the case, this illustration was deliberately designed to show that the lowest price does not necessarily win the contract. Firm B's proposal had passed the rated evaluation and was the lowest cost.

However, once quality (rated evaluation) and price were factored together, Firm B's rank is third place when the evaluation of price per point is done.

This illustration also shows that the highest quality proposal does not necessarily win the contract. The firm with the highest quality proposal was firm C.

Firm A, with the lowest price per point, received the contract. As it happens, Firm A was not the lowest price or the highest quality.

A quality proposal is always critical. However as the next two examples will show, you have to judge how much quality to build into your proposal.

This illustration also demonstrates the importance of preparing a proposal carefully. Every point gained with your proposal helps increase your odds of winning the contract.

Method 2: Total Points - Proposal and Price

Another method is to have two completely separate evaluations. The rated evaluation and the price evaluation are calculated separately with each receiving a separate point rating. The two calculations are then totaled together and the contract is awarded to the firm receiving the highest total points.

As with method 1, the goal is still to blend quality (rated evaluation) with price

In the following case, the decision was made to have the final score out of 100. As quality was deemed to be paramount over price, the points were weighted in favour of quality. The Rated Evaluation (quality) received a maximum of 75 points and the financial proposal (price) received a maximum of 25 points.

The pass mark for the rated evaluation was set at 70 out of 100 and three firms qualified after that evaluation was done.

For the purposes of demonstrating the difference in the methodologies, the same three firms will be used with the same rated scores and total prices.

Firm	Total Evaluated Points /100	Total Dollars
A	80	$105,000.00
B	71	$ 99,000.00
C	85	$115,000.00

With the rated evaluation out of 75, it is necessary to recalculate the points. The above points were out of 100.

Therefore the formula to adjust the evaluated total is:

$$\frac{\text{Total Points Available}}{\text{Total Evaluated Points}} \times \frac{75}{100} = \text{Adjusted Total}$$

The adjusted totals for each firm are as follows:

Firm A – 80 x 75/100 = 60 points
Firm B – 71 x 75/100 = 53.25 points
Firm C – 85 x 75/100 = 63.75 points

The next calculation necessary is the financial calculation. The total number of points available are 25. Therefore, the lowest total price quotation receives 25 points. In this case, Firm B with a price of $99,000 is the lowest price. The other prices are calculated relative to the lowest price.

The formula for calculating the points for the price is:

$$\frac{\text{Lowest Total Price Bid}}{\text{Total Price Bid by Firm}} \times 25 = \text{Financial Evaluated Points}$$

When this is done, the price total points for each firm are
Firm A – 23.57 points
Firm B – 25 points (full marks due to lowest price)
Firm C – 21.52 points.

The only item remaining is to total the points together to determine the winning proposal.

Firm	Total Rated Points	Total Financial Points	Total Points
A	60	23.57	83.57
B	53.25	25	78.25
C	63.75	21.52	85.27*

*winning proposal

The highest total points obtained are Firm C and this firm would receive the contract.

The above methodology is used mainly when a decision is made that quality resulting is more important than the price.

It is informative to look back to Method 1: Price Per Point as a comparison. Exactly the same scores were used in each example. However, due to the differing methodology the results are different.

Using Price Per Point, the winning proposal was submitted by Firm A. Using Total Points, the winning proposal was submitted by Firm C. Knowing how your proposal will be assessed is vitally important information that will help guide you in preparing your proposal.

Method 3: Lowest Priced Responsive Bid

The Lowest Priced Responsive Bid is another method of determining who will get a contract.

This method has been around for years and, until recently, had been gradually disappearing. With bid challenges becoming common in the public sector, it has enjoyed a revival. The public sector finds it easier to defend its evaluation of bids when it only has to explain the price.

As with both method 1 and 2, the goal is still to ensure that there is a quality (rated evaluation) proposal. However in this case, price is much more important. All firms who meet the minimum evaluation threshold are considered equal and the final evaluation is based strictly on price.

As with the previous methods, the pass mark for the rated evaluation was set at 70 out of 100 and three firms qualified after that evaluation was done.

Once again, for the purposes of demonstrating the difference in the methodologies, the same three firms will be used with the same rated scores and total prices.

Firm	Total Evaluated Points	Total Dollars
A	80/100	$105,000.00
B	71/100	$ 99,000.00*
C	85/100	$115,000.00

* winning proposal

Using Lowest Priced Responsive Bid, the answer becomes straightforward. The goal was to find a firm that could do the job with an acceptable quality.

Since all three firms A, B and C received more than 70 points and met the rated evaluation minimum criteria there bids are considered equivalent even though there is a large difference in their evaluation with Firm B receiving only 71 points compared to Firms A and C receiving 80 and 85 points respectively. .

We next turn to the total bid price for the firms and select the Lowest Priced proposal. This is firm B with a total bid price of

$99,000.00.

Analysis

The above three method of evaluation proposals are not the only methods that are available. However they are commonly used.

The examples were chosen carefully to illustrate the importance of understanding how the proposal will be assessed. Using exactly the same rated and financial results for all three methods resulted in three different winners.

To summarize:

- Method 1 – Lowest Price Per Point – Used for an RFP when a blending of quality and price is the desired outcome.
- Method 2 – Total Points – Used for an RFP when the quality of the proposal is considered more important than the price.
- Method 3 – Lowest Priced Responsive Bid – Used for an RFP when price is an important factor and the quality only needs to meet a minimum.

Variations

It is fair and important to mention that there is a variation in the method of evaluating rated requirements that needs to be watched for. It is possible that, instead of stating only a pass mark of 70% (or 80%, or whatever was decided by the customer) the RFP evaluation criteria also states that certain sections within the evaluation must have minimum scores as well.

For example, if the RFP states the proposal must receive 70% overall this means that you can receive from 0 to 100% in any section as long as the 70% overall is obtained. But a lower or higher minimum score may be set for one or more other sections in an RFP. This means that you might get 70% overall but still fail if you are under the minimum in one or more specific sections.

18. Questions

During the RFP process, you can ask the procurement officer questions regarding the RFP. In order to know what to ask, you need to analyze the RFP closely. Questions are important. During the bid period, through asking the right questions, an apparently biased RFP can be amended and become neutral.

Questions concerning all elements of the RFP can occur anytime during the bid process. For example, the initial review of the RFP by the Red Team may reveal contradictory dates, a need for clarifications, confusion as to the duration of the contract, evaluation points not adding up to the correct total and/or the pricing basis needs amending.

Other questions will develop over time as the Preparation Team starts writing the response to the RFP. Additionally, answers to questions that were submitted earlier or amendments to the RFP can create even more questions. In fact, the range and subject of the questions are too great and varied to itemize as a problem could exist in any aspect of the RFP.

Some customers issue RFPs which are vague and confusing. Questions are an excellent way of providing focus and clarifying what is expected. Consider the purpose of your question and what you want in the response. You must then write and submit the question.

There are two important elements associated with questions – "What to ask" and "How to ask it."

Finally, you have to decide if you want to ask the question. The Red Team and Proposal Preparation Team are doing their work correctly if they identify questions that should be asked. However, you may feel that you already know the answer and therefore you don't want to lose what might be a competitive advantage. Since answers are sent to all potential bidders, the question might reveal a weakness in your firm that competitors could exploit, or give competitors other information that you don't want them to have.

The answers to the questions can, in many cases, provide enlightening insight into "what they really want." It also serves as a benchmark on what the other companies are thinking.

Questions should be carefully crafted so that a predetermined answer or a clarification is forced from the customer. The question, "Do you still contract or re-employ pensioners who used to work full-time in your office through temporary help agencies?" is a good example of this type of question. Of course the answer cannot be "Yes". Equally, it cannot be "No" due to the word "still". To answer this question, the client is forced to provide a written explanation. Writing the question carefully avoids vague answers and wasted time.

Warning: Many RFPs limit the time period during which questions are allowed. This has to be factored into the development of the proposal so that important questions can be asked. Mark it down as a milestone in project planning.

When you receive the answers to questions, do an immediate analysis. The answers can add insight into what is wanted. In some cases the answer may contradict information contained elsewhere in the RFP. The answers can also cause you to ask further questions.

In many cases, the answers will cause a rewrite of what has already been written for your proposal. While it takes up valuable time, it is time well spent. This will improve your proposal and increase your odds of winning the contract.

Always be specific when asking questions. Help make it easy for

Questions

the client to know where to look in the RFP. Always reference the RFP page, clause number, and paragraph number. Number your questions for easy of reference.

For example:

Q1.
Re. Pg 3, para 4, Conflict of Interest.
The RFP calls for independent contractors to the main contractor to be identified. Please explain the rationale for this request.

Q2
Re. Pg 14, preamble, Basis of Payment
The RFP calls for the inclusion of training facitilies (page 4, para 2), but the Basis of Payment does not provide for costing this expense. Please amend the Basis of Payment.

19. Debriefings

A debriefing is feedback from the customer on the proposal that you submitted in response to the RFP. The officials debriefing you are normally the buyer and at least one representative of the evaluation team. It is treated as a very formal meeting and to avoid arguments or bid challenges, discussion will normally be limited to the strengths and weaknesses in your proposal, the anticipated responses and how you were scored in relation to the evaluation criteria.

Whether your proposal wins and you receive a contract or whether you are unsuccessful, you should always request a debriefing. The only way to get better is to learn your strengths, weaknesses and the areas that need improving. The best time to request a debriefing is during the bid period before you submit the proposal for consideration. At that time, a commitment on a face to face meeting is easier to obtain. Be certain to convey to the buyer that you are bidding with the expectation of winning and that win or lose, you still expect to obtain a detailed, comprehensive, candid de-brief of how your proposal was evaluated.

As the winner, the debriefing will help you by letting you know where you were weak in your submission. In that way, your next proposal can be stronger. Also, as the winner, the debriefing comments may be more open and less formal since, obviously, you are not going to argue with or challenge the results. An additional benefit may be learning that you lost marks in areas where you thought that you had given solid information. In other words, you were weak where you thought that you were strong.

For the unsuccessful firm, there are two reasons to request a debriefing. First you may have been classified as non-responsive. The debriefing will help you learn where you made critical errors. Second, it may be that you did not submit a strong enough proposal. In either event, as with the winner, the debriefing will help you learn the weak points in your submission and help you win more RFPs in the future.

When attending a debriefing session, take along at least one person who is designated to be a listener and recorder. Normally, you will not be allowed to tape the conversation. It is an advantage if you have a person who does not participate in the discussion as the debriefing occurs. This will ensure that careful notes of key points of the conversation will be taken.

There are many factors to consider during a debriefing and the following is a guideline only.

How to conduct yourself during a Debriefing:

- Do not act defensively
- Attitude should be how to improve in the future
- Be curious
- Calmly accept the results
- Smile

What To Do or Not to Do:

- Do, before the debriefing, prepare questions that you would like answered
- Do ask questions focused on lessons learned
- Do ensure that you understand evaluation
- Do not accept generalities or partial explanations
- Do insist on full explanations and details
- Do not hesitate to ask for more details on how you were scored
- Do ask how you could do better in the future

Debriefings

- Do ask how you could improve your proposal generally through better writing, graphics, etc.
- Do take extensive notes of what is said

What to ask during the debriefing, whether you know the answer or not.

- Who won?
- Did the incumbent win?
- How many bidders were there?
- What was the total value of the contract?
- What were your total points in the rated evaluation?
- Where did you lose points in the rated evaluation?
- Where did you gain points in the rated evaluation?
- Was your price the lowest price?
- Was your level of effort (people assigned) adequate?
- How was the presentation of your proposal?

After the debriefing, hold an immediate meeting with the people who attended the debriefing and prepare a summary. In this way, important information conveyed will not get lost or forgotten.

The following questions should be asked during this session and during the "lessons learned" meeting.

- Can you apply the information to other RFPs in the future?
- Did we interpret the RFP correctly?
- What other questions should we have asked at the debriefing?
- Did we make a preventable error in preparing the proposal?
- Are there changes necessary to our proposal development process?
- Do we need better training in preparing proposals?
- Should we hire professionals to help prepare proposals in the future?

- Are there any suggestions to improve our performance?

After this has been done, the following day (or a couple of days later) hold a "lessons learned" meeting with all members of the Proposal Team and the Red Team. Allow people to ask questions regarding what has been learned. The reason for the delay is to allow a "cooling off" period so that you can focus on what has been said, rather than how you feel.

Communicate what you have learned to your proposal team. Team members who worked hard to create a winning proposal deserve to hear positive feedback about their help in winning the bid. By the same token, team members who worked hard to create a proposal which was unsuccessful, need to know the negative feedback and points to consider for future proposals.

Annex A

Request for Information/Letter of Interest

This Annex contains a Request for Information (RFI) so that the reader can understand and visualize how a RFI is presented and the information requested.

This was an actual RFI that was used. Some minor information that would not affect the analysis has been amended or deleted, such as the name of the organization and details that would identify the user.

The commentary in italics and parenthesizes was not part of the original RFI and has been inserted to help understand the RFI.

Example 1 – RFI for Sports Referee Services

(This RFI was issued by the federal government)

Sports referee services

This letter of interest is not an invitation to bid. No contract will be awarded as a result of this letter. (*This is important. The buying organization is informing you that this is not a contractual document).*

The Minister of ABC requires the services of a contractor specializing in official refereeing of various sports in order to provide the services described below, according to an established schedule as well as on request and as required.
(In one sentence you are being informed of the purpose of the RFI. If this is not your specialty then you can stop reading.)

How to Respond to a RFP
Understanding the Bid and Proposal Process

Sports:
The services covered herein concern the following sports: hockey, broomball, ball hockey, slow-pitch, volleyball and soccer.

Services:
During the term/duration of the contract, the contractor will be responsible for providing the staff required to deliver the requested services by performing duties that include, but are not strictly limited to, the following:
-    Creating and maintaining a call-up list of individuals available upon request and duly qualified to act as official referees for each of the sports listed herein;
-    Determining and assigning the number of qualified individuals required to perform the duties in question according to the established schedule and upon request;
-    Performing official referee and timekeeping duties at every game or match according to the schedule provided;
-    Gathering and recording data, updating charts and managing statistics according to the established format; and
-    Training referees and line/goal judges in "clinics" at the beginning of the season and for the term of the contract.

Scope:

(As you read the Scope, you will realize that the information is not provided in any detail. You are being provided mainly with an outline and input is being sought regarding this initiative. In many sports organizations, referees can only work on sanctioned games. There is nothing in this document to indicate that even an initial investigation has been done on the refereeing issue.)

Annex A
Request for Information/Letter of Interest

Services will be provided upon request and as required only.
- An activity schedule (games or matches) for each of the aforementioned sports will be given to the contractor before the beginning of the season.

Locations:
- Depending on the season, the sports specified herein will be played on-site at XYZ facitity/.

Schedule:
- Except in special circumstances, the intramural sports specified herein will take place during the week, Monday to Thursday inclusively, from 4:00 pm to 10:00 pm inclusively, from October 1 to mid-April for the majority and until September 30 for slow-pitch;
- The maximum length of any game or match is approximately two (2) hours.

Personnel required:
- Head referee;
- Referee in charge;
- "Federated" referee;
- Line or goal judge;
- Scorekeeper/timekeeper.

Approximate number of games/matches annually:
- Hockey 250;
- Ball hockey 70;
- Volleyball 36;
- Broomball 50;
- Slow-pitch 50;
- Soccer 370.

No price is required for this letter of interest. Department ABC is seeking to determine suppliers' interest in providing this type of service. Potential suppliers are asked to submit their comments on the requested services and indicate their interest in providing this service.

(You are being informed that they are looking for suppliers who can provide the services. They are also not certain that any supplier can provide a complete service. Comments received may indicate that different organizations handled by different sports should undertake the work).

Your comments/replies must be received by the closing date given in the notice. Send your comments/replies to:
Attention: *(name withheld)*

(You have just been told that no suggestions or further input on potential solutions will be considered after the closing date. The RFI used the word "must". This is the standard bureaucratic wording. The statement would have been better if they had said, "Your comments/replies are requested by..." As this is only "Request" for information, input after the official closing date that was of value would still be considered.)

If you have any questions, feel free to contact the above named procurement officer.
Delivery Date: Above-mentioned

The Crown retains the right to negotiate with suppliers on any procurement.

(This statement is confusing. The second sentence in the RFI stated, "No contract will be awarded as a result of this letter." However, it did not say that they would not open negotiations with a firm to develop a contract as a result of the RFI.)

(You need to develop clarity and therefore, you should ask the procurement officer in writing whether they intend to negotiate with a firm who responds to the RFI or issue a subsequent competitive RFP.)

Annex A
Request for Information/Letter of Interest

(Finally, if you are interested in eventually submitting a proposal but do not have time to develop a response, sent a letter indicating your interest. In this way it if they receive input from only one firm, the client cannot assume there are no other firms who can potentially offer the service.)

ANNEX B

Advance Contract Award Notice (ACAN)

This Annex has ACANs presented in full. This is done so that you can understand and visualize how an ACAN may be presented.

The following were actual ACANs. Some changes have been made to the names, numbers and content in all the following examples to obscure the original service that was being sole sourced. Other than these changes, the presentation and information remains as it appeared on the electronic tendering board. In particular, the most important item, the reason for non-competitive bidding has remained intact.

As you read them, think about the following question, "Could this ACAN be challenged? Why? " This question will be asked and answered at the end of the ACAN.

The commentary in italics AND parenthesizes that appears was not part of the original RFP and has been inserted for better understanding.

ACAN 1

TITLE: Contract and Requisition Reporting System (CRRS) - Systems Testing and Training Officer.

1. The purpose and explanation of an ACAN

An Advance Contract Award Notice (ACAN) allows the Department of ABC contracting authorities to post a notice on

How to Respond to a RFP
Understanding the Bid and Proposal Process

MERX, for no less than fifteen (15) calendar days, indicating to the supplier community that a good, service or construction contract will be awarded to a pre-identified contractor. If no other supplier submits, on or before the closing date, a Statement of Capabilities that meets the requirements set out in the ACAN, the contracting authority may then proceed with the award. However, should a Statement of Capabilities be found to meet the requirements set out in the ACAN, then the contracting authority will proceed to a full tendering process.

(MERX is one of the well known electronic bulletin boards and can be found at www.Merx.com. The Department is advising all potential suppliers of the potential bidding opportunity.)

2. Rights of suppliers

Suppliers who believe that they are fully qualified and available to provide the services or goods described in this ACAN may submit a Statement of Capabilities clearly demonstrating how they meet the advertised requirement. This Statement of Capabilities must be provided via e-mail only to the contact person identified in Section 12 of this Notice on or before the closing date and time of the Notice. If there is a reasonable level of evidence regarding capability, the requirements will be opened to electronic or traditional bidding processes.

(Only a supplier who could bid has "rights". If you read this and decided that you could not supply the service, then you have no rights – even if you realized that there was an error in the rationale for sole source.)

3. Proposed Contractor

XYZ Inc, Ottawa, Ontario, Canada

(It is a requirement that if the decision is to sole source, then all potential suppliers have to be advised who is the intended

Annex B
Advance Contract Award Notice (ACAN)

supplier.)

4.   Definition of Requirements or Expected Results

The MRS – Management and Reporting System - is a business critical system used by Department ABC to manage workflow for all contract review cycles. The system was built through integration of a unique combination of four different technologies. The application is accessed through the department's intranet via a web browser.

MRS is adding new functionality and improvements which are designed to meet the current business requirements of the department. Specific technical and operational expertise in MRS is required to allow user testing for acceptance, to provide client assistance and support, and to provide training to new users, management and new members of the MRS team. The successful day-to-day operation of the system is dependant upon obtaining and retaining this expertise.

5. Minimum requirements

The minimum requirements for this requirement are identified as follows:
a) The ability to begin productive work as of the contract start date.
b) Knowledge of Department ABC's current Branch and Regional structures.
c) Knowledge of MRS operations and workflows from technical and client perspectives.
d) User Acceptance Testing methodology.
e) Provision of client systems training in the operation of the MRS application.

(Considerable thought has been given into the minimum requirements necessary for the service to be provided.)

6. Reason for non-competitive award

Section 6(d) of the Government Contracts Regulations states that only one person is capable of performing the work. This exception is being invoked because Department ABC believes that XYZ Inc. is the only contracting resource capable of providing the work in the required time frame. The Department's reasons are as follows:

a) The integration of four separate technologies, have been used to create MRS. This unique application in that it uses an integration of as mentioned above. The department believes that XYZ Inc. has demonstrated his understanding and familiarity of this technology through his previous work with technology products.

b) XYZ Inc. has the required knowledge of Department ABC's current Branch and Regional structures as they apply to the operations of MRS. Based on previous work on a number of projects, it has the demonstrated experience to explain MRS functionality to clients, new users, management and new members which will allow XYZ Inc. to immediately begin working on the next phase of this project.

c) Based on work undertaken on a number of previous career projects XYZ Inc. has demonstrated the required background technical knowledge to immediately begin MRS testing, provide MRS client support, and conduct MRS training sessions as required. Failure to retain any of this assistance in a timely manner would place the timeline of MRS development and testing at risk, would jeopardize MRS training schedules and negatively impact client support and day-to-day operations.

7. Applicable trade agreements and justification for limited tendering or the Procurement: North American Free Trade Agreement (NAFTA); Agreement on Internal Trade (AIT); World Trade Organization - Agreement on Government Procurement

Annex B
Advance Contract Award Notice (ACAN)

(WTO-AGP).

8. Ownership of Intellectual Property

Intellectual property arising from the performance of the work under the contract as a result of this ACAN will vest with the Contractor.

9. Period of the proposed contract

The contract period shall be from date of contract award until March 31, 2010, with right to renew for a one year option.

10. Estimated value of the proposed contract

The total estimated value of the proposed contract should not exceed $400,000.00, including travel and living expenses (if applicable), and all applicable taxes.

(It is not clear if the $400,000 is for the period till March 31, 2010 or if it includes the option period. The total amount might be $800,000 if the option year was added.)

11. Closing date and time

The closing date and time for accepting Statements of Capabilities is, August 14, 2008 at 2 p.m. EST.

12. Contact Person

All inquiries with regard to this Notice must be addressed by e-mail to: Mr. A. Nonymous

The Question: "Could the ACAN be challenged? Why?"

This ACAN can probably be challenged. The statement used in the justification is, "This exception is being invoked because Department ABC believes that XYZ Inc. is the only contracting resource capable of providing the work in the required time frame." A belief is not a valid rationale. There must be facts to substantiate the firm having the "exclusive" knowledge.

Furthermore, the department gave three reasons why they decided to sole source:

a) Previous experience working with the department is not allowable as a justification for sole sourcing. Any other supplier can gain his knowledge should they be given the opportunity to work with the department

b) same justification as for a)

c) same justification as for a) but added urgency. Urgency in this case would be poor planning and is not a valid reason for sole sourcing.

Annex B
Advance Contract Award Notice (ACAN)

ACAN 2

Title: Specialized Negotiation Support Services – Standing Offer

1.   Purpose of an Advance Contract Award Notice (ACAN)

An Advance Contract Award Notice (ACAN) allows a department to post a notice, for no less than fifteen calendar days, indicating to the supplier community that it intends to award a contract to a pre-identified contractor. If no other supplier submits, during the fifteen calendar day posting period, a statement of capabilities that meets the requirements set out in the ACAN, the competitive requirements of the government's contracting policy have been met. Following notification to suppliers not successful in demonstrating that their statement of capabilities meets the requirements set out in the ACAN, the contract may then be awarded using the Treasury Board's electronic bidding authorities.

(The organization is advising all potential suppliers of the potential bidding opportunity.)

If other potential suppliers submit statements of capabilities during the fifteen calendar day posting period, and meet the requirements set out in the ACAN, the department must proceed to a full tendering process on either the government's electronic tendering service or through traditional means, in order to award the contract."

(Note the difference in the wording between ACAN #1 and ACAN #2. While the wording is different due to a different organization issuing the RFI, the intent is the same.)

2.   Definition of Requirements

On an as and when required basis, the KNobbly Knee Division of the Department ABC requires specialized research, analysis and planning support for several on-going claims and specific negotiations, where knees are an issue, in Alberta and in British Columbia.

In order to provide the required services, the Contractor must have extensive experience in the negotiation of Funny Knee claims and specific claims, in particular, the negotiations of claims where water on the knee is affected. Also, the Contractor must have the necessary technical expertise in appraisal and valuation studies, compensation models for knees, and third party dispositions to provide the factual and analytical support required to develop and to implement negotiation strategies. The Contractor must have the knowledge of and experience with policies and procedures in regard to specific knee negotiations, considered essential requirements to adequately support complex negotiations.

The contractor must have secret security clearance.

3.   Governing Contracting Rules

This procurement is subject to the North American Free Trade Agreement (NAFTA) and the Agreement on Internal Trade (AIT).

4.   Ownership of Intellectual Property

The Department of Old Knees has determined that any intellectual property arising from the performance of the work under the contract will vest with Canada, on the following grounds: statutes, regulations or prior obligations of Canada to a third party or parties preclude Contractor ownership of the Intellectual Property Rights in Foreground Information.

Annex B
Advance Contract Award Notice (ACAN)

5.   Period of Proposed Standing Offer
Commencement Date: February 2, 2012
Completion Date: January 31, 2013(with two additional one year options)

6.   Estimated Value of Proposed Standing Offer
$ 500,000.00 including the option years.

7.   Reason for non-competitive award

a)   Article 1016: 2(b) and 2(d) of the North American Free Trade Agreement and Article 506: 12 a) and b) of the Agreement on Internal Trade.

b)   Knee Knocking Inc (Mr. Tom Townsend) is considered uniquely suited to continue to perform the proposed standing offer work. Mr. Townsend was a member of the federal negotiation team that settled the Water on the Knee claim and, as such, is uniquely qualified to support negotiations, where water on the knee interests are affected. Mr. Townsend has also participated in the negotiation of settlements with Knee Joke plagiarism in Alberta, which involved water on the knees. In addition, he was engaged to help develop strategies to facilitate negotiations and has an extensive knowledge of the issues associated with those negotiations. Currently a key member of the federal negotiation team for the Foot in Mouth specific claims, Mr. Townsend's continued participation in the negotiation is considered essential to their successful conclusion.

The proposed contractor has the required combination of experience in the negotiation of specific claims and bony knee claims, in particular the negotiations of claims where water on the knee interests are affected. Having been a member of several negotiating teams that have settled specific claims in the past, he also has the necessary technical expertise as it pertains to providing the factual and analytical support required to develop and implement negotiation strategies and to work with the Knobbly Knee Division of the Department. His knowledge of and experience with policies and procedures in regard to specific negotiations are also considered essential requirements. He is the only known individual who has the required background knowledge and experience to adequately continue to support complex negotiations.

8. Proposed Contractor
Knee Knocking Inc. Alberta

(It is a requirement that if the decision is to sole source, then all potential suppliers have to be advised who is the intended supplier)

9. Submission of Statement of Capabilities by Suppliers:

Suppliers, who consider themselves fully qualified and available to provide the services described herein, may submit a statement of capabilities in writing to the contact person identified in this Notice on or before the closing date of this Notice. The statement of capabilities must clearly demonstrate how the supplier meets the advertised requirements.

10. Closing Date for Submission of Statements of Capabilities

15:00 hour Eastern Daylight Saving Time, (December 2, 20120.

11. Departmental Contact Person

Suppliers may inquire or submit a statement of capabilities to:
Ms. U. N. Known
Purchasing Division,
Department ABC

The Question: "Could the ACAN be challenged? Why?"

This ACAN appears to be valid. There is a unique combination of experience needed and only the one individual possesses it.

However it is somewhat unclear where the contractor gained his knowledge and you may want to ask a question about this. If the knowledge was gained working on earlier contracts for the department then the experience (and the sole source justification) may be challengeable.

Annex C

Case Study - RFP Example

The following is an example of an RFP presented in full. This is to help you analyze and understand the RFP process.

This RFP was actually used with the format and content below. Changes have been made to names and numbers. The changes to the subject matter illustrate that the Red Team review and questions do not depend on technical expertise. While it may occur in various cases, it is not necessary.

The Red Team's expertise is procurement and the process. As such, the Red Team should be able to review almost any RFP and proposal. In fact, a lack of in-depth subject matter expertise helps the Red Team avoid errors by ensuring the Red Team remains focused on their task.

It is suggested that you analyze the following proposal and make comments regarding oversights, changes, errors or questions that need to be sent to the client. You will notice that there are many "boilerplate" clauses that are in the RFP.

The key place to focus on is the Statement of Work (SOW) and the Evaluation Criteria which are customized for each RFP.

Following the RFP, is a example of a Red Team analysis of the RFP containing questions that the Red Team may suggest need to be asked for clarification of the RFP. The presentation of the Red Team review can change, depending on the author, but the information remains intact.

Note that the Red Team always writes a separate report with references. The Red Team never edits or writes on any original documentation. This hold true for both the proposal and the RFP.

The commentary in italics and parenthesizes that appears was not part of the original RFP and has been inserted for better understanding.

REQUEST FOR PROPOSAL

TITLE: STRATEGIC ADVICE ON MAINTAINING THE STATUS QUO

REFERENCE NUMBER G. D.

SOLICITATION CLOSING DATE: **September 31, 2012** (2:00 p.m.) EASTERN DAYLIGHT SAVING TIME (E.D.T.)

ADDRESS INQUIRIES TO CONTRACTING AUTHORITY:
Mr. N. Sense

SEND PROPOSAL TO:
STATUS QUO CANADA
MAIL AND DISTRIBUTION SERVICES
OTTAWA

THE FOLLOWING SECTION MUST BE FILLED BY CONTRACTOR:
CONTRACTOR'S NAME:
CONTRACTOR'S ADDRESS:
NAMES & TITLE OF PERSON AUTHORIZED TO SIGN ON BEHALF OF CONTRACTOR (PLEASE PRINT):

SIGNATURE:
(THE SIGNATURE INDICATES ACCEPTANCE OF THE TERMS AND CONDITIONS SET OUT HEREIN)
DATE:_____

THIS PAGE MUST BE COMPLETED AND INCLUDED WITH YOUR TECHNICAL PROPOSAL

SECTION "A" PROPOSAL INSTRUCTIONS

1. RECEIPT OF PROPOSALS:

For this solicitation, copies of sealed bids must be presented and must clearly be marked with the supplier's name, address, bid solicitation number, closing date and time

2. SUBMISSION OF PROPOSAL:

PROPOSALS ARE TO BE SUBMITTED UTILISING A TWO ENVELOPE SYSTEM

ENVELOPE 1 – TECHNICAL PROPOSAL

2.1 Bidders must submit 3 copies of the Technical Proposal
a) No financial information is to be included in envelope 1.
b) Technical Proposal (First page of the Request for Proposal (RFP) duly completed and signed.
c) All certifications in Section "F" completed and signed

ENVELOPE 2 – FINANCIAL PROPOSAL

2.2 Bidders must submit 1 copy of the Financial Proposal

a) No technical information is to be included in envelope 2.

NOTE: Both Envelopes must be presented and clearly marked with the following:

How to Respond to a RFP
Understanding the Bid and Proposal Process

• the supplier's name and address;
• the bid solicitation number;
• closing time and date;

PROPOSALS MUST BE RECEIVED AT THE FOLLOWING
ADDRESS:
Status Quo Canada
Mail and Distribution Services
Ottawa, Ontario

• Courier and By Hand deliveries are accepted between 7:30 and
16:30 Monday through Friday except on Government holidays.

• Late proposals submitted by facsimile or e-mail will be rejected.

*(This is an important point to note. Late proposals submitted by
facsimile or e-mail will be rejected. Does this mean that
proposals on time if submitted by facsimile or e-mail will be
accepted. We can only read on to find the answer.)*

NOTICE: Due to the nature of this Request for Proposal,
electronic transmission of offer by such means as electronic mail
or facsimile to the Status Quo Canada (SQC) is not considered
to be practical and therefore will not be accepted. The offer
MUST be delivered to the Bidding Receiving Unit, by the time
and date indicated on page 1 of this Request for Proposal.

*(We now have the answer to the first question. Proposals
submitted by facsimile or e-mail will not be accepted. This is
typical of RFPs. This is an excellent example. The RFP could
have simply said, "...Electronic mail or facsimile are not
acceptable..." Instead it has statements that could cause
confusion. If you had not read carefully, you may have
interpreted the first statement to mean that proposals submitted
on time would be accepted by e-mail or facsimile would be
acceptable.)*

Annex C
Case Study – RFP Example

TIMELY AND CORRECT DELIVERY OF BIDS TO THE SPECIFIED BID DELIVERY ADDRESS IS THE SOLE RESPONSIBILITY OF THE BIDDER. STATUS QUO CANADA WILL NOT ASSUME SUCH RESPONSIBILITY UNDER ANY CIRCUMSTANCES. THE BIDDER ASSUMES ALL RISKS AND/OR CONSEQUENCES RESULTING FROM AN INCORRECT BID DELIVERY.

3. PRESENTATION OF PROPOSAL

3.1 It is requested that proposals follow the following response format / instructions:
a) use 8 ½" x 11" bond paper; and
b) use a numbering system corresponding to the Request for Proposal (RFP)
and statement of work
c) submit a proposal no more than 10 pages in length.

(By use of the word "requested" at 3.1 instead of must, the decision on how to present the proposal is left to the bidder. You cannot be penalized for deviating from this))

3.2 It must also include:
a) all references to descriptive material, technical manuals and brochures;
b) the signed Bidder/Price Certificate – SECTION F; and
c) the first page of the RFP.

Bidder's proposal must include the first page of this RFP properly completed and signed.

(At 3.2, the RFP states "must". Therefore everything above has to be included. This qualifies as a "hidden mandatory".)

The signature indicates acceptance of the terms and conditions set out herein. Ensure that the signatory has the authority to commit the Bidder by making such a contractual offer.

4. RIGHTS OF THE CROWN

During the evaluation, representatives of the Crown may, at their discretion:

4.1 Seek clarification or obtain verification of statements made in a proposal;

4.2 Cancel and/or re-issue this RFP at any time;

4.3 Verify any or all information provided by the Bidder with respect to this RFP including references;

4.4 Retain all proposals submitted in response to this RFP.

5. REVISIONS

Revisions must be submitted in writing and must be received before the closing date and time.

(It can and does happen that amendments to RFPs are issued with changes at the last minute. Also, firms when rechecking their information, discover mistakes that were made. If the firm has already submitted its proposal, it can submit a revision to this proposal before the closing time.)

6. ACCEPTANCE

SQC will not necessarily accept the lowest bid, or any of the proposals submitted.

7. LEVEL OF DETAILS

The proposal must be submitted in sufficient detail to form the basis of a contractual agreement and shall include:

7.1 A summary of the firm's experience especially in areas related to the work requirements.

7.2 The identification of any tasks which are felt to be important but not mentioned in the Statement of Work.

7.3 Contractors must guarantee price quotations for 90 days.

Annex C
Case Study – RFP Example

(7. is giving general instructions. The only important point is that the price has to be guaranteed for 90 days. That means that you can not withdraw or cancel your bid.)

8. OTHER REQUIREMENTS

Proposals must be submitted in accordance with these instructions and/or those contained in the Statement of Work;
8.1 By responding to this RFP, the Contractor confirms his/her understanding that failure to comply with any of the conditions herein will result in the rejection of the submission.
8.2 There shall be no direct payment by the Crown for costs incurred for the presentation and submission of proposals in response to this RFP.

(This clause is simply stating that the cost of preparing your proposal is not chargeable.)

8.3 In case of addition errors in the financial document, the unit price of each element of the contract will be added together to produce the overall cost of the bid.

(This clause explains generally how the client will evaluate your financial proposal. Detailed information should be further on in the RFP.)

8.4 After the proposal closing date and time, no amendments will be accepted.
8.5 Notwithstanding that they have not been expressly articulated in this RFP, the standard instructions, general terms, conditions and clauses relating to consulting and professional services (obtained by Federal Government Departments) will apply to any contract resulting from this RFP. The Contractor agrees, by submitting his proposal, to all the above Terms and Conditions.

(This clause states that when you submit your proposal, all the

terms and conditions in this RFP become binding on the bidder. (This includes the clauses and conditions that were included by reference. It is the bidder's responsibility to look up these clauses.

(There is no allowance for discussion. This illustrates the importance of reading the RFP carefully and when it is issued. Any problems with the Terms or Conditions have to be addressed to your lawyer and with the client before the RFP closing date.)

9. REFERENCES – CLARIFICATIONS

SQC reserves the right, before awarding the contract, to require the Contractor to submit such evidence of qualifications as SQC may deem necessary, and will consider evidence concerning the financial, technical and other qualifications and abilities of the Contractor.

SQC also reserves the right to request clarifications on the proposal.

(Negotiations normally take place with the recommended bidder only. Clarifications can take place with any bidder. The difference, in non-legal terms, is negotiations may result in changing the proposal while clarifications only give more information to support existing statements.)

10. ENQUIRIES

10.1 It is the Contractor's responsibility to completely understand the requirements and the instructions specified hereto. In the event that clarification is necessary, the contractor shall direct his/her concerns to the Contracting Authority ONLY BY e-mail or facsimile. NO VERBAL QUESTIONS OR CONCERNS WILL BE ACCEPTED.

Annex C
Case Study – RFP Example

(This may not seem to make sense and possibly a question should be prepared and sent to the purchasing officer. The RFP is a document for bidders but 10.1 refers to a contractor.)

10.2 A bid solicitation will not be extended if it has not been requested within 6 days of the bid solicitation closing date. SQC reserves the right not to extend any solicitation.

10.3 SQC is not obligated to respond to any questions received within 6 days prior to the closing date.

(This is another point where the importance of reading the RFP early is illustrated. Part of the proposal writing timeline has to include the cut-off date for asking questions.)

10.4 Following contract award, bidders may contact the Contracting Authority for a debriefing opportunity.

(Whether your proposal wins the contract or not, you should always request a debriefing.)

12. BIDDER SUGGESTIONS DURING THE PERIOD OF THE RFP

Should the bidder consider that the specifications or Statement of Work (SOW) contained in this RFP can be improved technically or technologically, the bidder is invited to make suggestions, in writing, to the Contracting Authority named herein. The bidder must clearly outline the suggested improvement as well as the reason for the suggestion.

Suggestions which do not restrict the level of competition nor favour a particular bidder will be given consideration provided they are received by the Contracting Authority no later than six (6) days prior to the bid closing date specified herein. Canada reserves the right to accept or reject any or all suggestions.

(As before, this cut-off date has to appear in your proposal writing timeline. Furthermore, should you believe that the RFP has inadvertent or deliberate bias in favour of a competitor, questions can help level the playing field for bidding.)

SECTION "B"

TERMS OF REFERENCE / STATEMENT OF WORK

PROJECT TITLE: STRATEGIC ADVICE ON STATUS QUO RESEARCH

1 BACKGROUND:

SQC requires the services of one Status Quo specialist. The work requires broad expertise and detailed knowledge of:
- creative inaction and theories, principles, techniques, methods and practices;
- Government of Canada policies, guidelines and requirements with respect to Bureaucratic mismanagement and decisive delays;
- the Department's procedures for the approval, contracting and conduct of inactivity;
- project management techniques; and
- research industry standards and practices in relation to resisting calls for change.

2 OBJECTIVES:

To assist SQC with high workload demands on an "as required" basis.

3 STATEMENT OF WORK:

(This is the section that should have been read first. It gives you the knowledge of whether this is in your field of expertise, or not.)

Annex C
Case Study – RFP Example

3.1 To assist SQC's status quo research group in providing strategic advice related to the Department's ongoing pressure to change and the speed of change, in the Department's priority areas of Lifelong Job Security, Workplace Skills and the Labour Market.

3.2 To provide advice on the methodologies and techniques most appropriate and cost effective for the Department's status quo research requirements, including advice on collection instruments, evaluation of final reports of studies, preparation and distribution of summary findings and secondary analysis of reports on the Department's issues.

3.3 To organize, plan and oversee the implementation of research projects. The activities could include direct contact with departmental clients, administrative staff, government officials responsible for the approval, coordination and contracting of creative and innovative inaction methodologies and projects. It could also include the preparation of reports, in multiple versions and presentation of research results.

4 CONTRACT PERIOD:

From date of contract award until October 30, 2012.

5 DELIVERABLES:

The deliverables may include research design and management services and may include any or all of the following, but not limited to:

a) Planning and design of research :
• Participation in discussion on research requirements / studies with departmental clients and with SQC officials;
• Provision of advice on research methodologies;
• Provision of advice on interview schedules and how to delay them

• Review of research reports, including version creation.

b) Preparation of research summaries and documentation for internal consideration of upcoming research projects:
• Preparation of briefing notes on the Department's efforts to maintain the status quo activities;
• Preparation of summaries of change management research findings that need correction.

6 BASIS OF PAYMENT:

Charges will be for professional time and invoices will be for actual hours worked and for on site meetings as required. Invoices for actual hours worked will be submitted on a monthly basis at the end of each month.

7 INTELLECTUAL PROPERTY:

Ownership of intellectual property will rest with the Crown.

8 OTHER CONSIDERATIONS:

Services may be provided in either official language.

The Contractor will work off-site but will be available for on-site meetings as required.

The Contractor will not provide information on any aspect of any proposed research directly or indirectly to any bidder or potential bidder either before or during any tendering process.

9 SECURITY LEVEL:

The Bidder must hold a valid security clearance at the level of ENHANCED RELIABILITY (RELIABILITY STATUS) prior to contract award. Bidders must provide confirmation of their level of security clearance. If a Bidder does not have the required security clearance, it may be obtained through SDC's Security office.

10 CONSTRAINT:

Budget (i.e.: budget maximum will not exceed $75,000.00 plus GST)

(This is important information to know. The cost of preparing a proposal may be significant. As a rule of thumb, the cost of preparing a proposal should be from 1 ½% of the expected value of the contract to, but no greater than, 5% which in this case is $3,750.00. What did the Bid/No Bid analysis indicate? Is the cost of preparing a proposal going to be greater than the potential profit if you win?)

SECTION "C" EVALUATION CRITERIA

MANDATORY REQUIREMENTS

(Section "C" and "D" are the sections that should have been read second. The Statement of Work let's you know if this is in your field of specialty. The Evaluation Criteria let's you know if you are able to bid or if there is a reasonable restriction on this ability.)

The mandatory requirements listed will be evaluated on a pass/fail (i.e. compliant / noncompliant) basis. Proposals that fail to meet the mandatory requirements will be disqualified at this stage without further consideration.

Proposals must demonstrate compliance with all of the following specifications and requirements and must provide the necessary documentation to support compliance in order to be considered.

BASIS OF SELECTION:

To be considered responsive, a bid must:

a) meet all the mandatory requirement of this solicitation; and,
b) obtain the required minimum of 60 percent of the points in EACH OF THE ITEM RATED requirement. The rating is performed on a scale of 70 points.
c) proposals not meeting a) and b) will not be given further consideration

Statement of Compliancy Requirement

M-1 The bidder's proposed individual MUST demonstrate, through education, experience or a combination of the two, a strong familiarity with both inaction and non-change management methodologies and techniques.

M-2 The bidder's proposed personnel MUST demonstrate at least two years experience within the last five years, working in a federal government department either as a contractor or an employee.

M-3 The bidder MUST submit a Curriculum Vitae for the proposed personnel.

M-4 The bidder MUST include, as part of the proposal, all requested documentation as requested under the Rated Criteria item no. 1.

M-5 Bidder must provide at least two verifiable references.

M-6 The bidder MUST be in compliance with the Certification requirements (see Section F of this RFP). The Certification forms **MUST** be duly completed and submitted at the time of submission.

Note: It is SQC courtesy to return, unopened, financial bids to the bidder which have note meet the mandatory criteria

SECTION "D" EVALUATION CRITERIA

Annex C
Case Study – RFP Example

RATED CRITERIA

(This is the continuation of the sections that should have been read second. The Statement of Work let's you know if this is in your field of specialty. The Evaluation Criteria let's you know if you are able to bid or if there is a reasonable restriction on this ability.)

1. RATED EVALUATION REQUIREMENTS

The criteria contained herein will be used by SQC to evaluate each Proposal.

Each Proposal will be evaluated according to the following criteria. Bidders are advised to address these requirements in the following order, where possible, and in sufficient depth in their proposals to enable a thorough assessment. An item not addressed will be given zero (0) points under the point rated system. SQC's assessment will be based solely on the information contained within the Proposal. SQC may seek further information or clarification from bidders. Only those proposals which achieve the highest Technical (60%) and Price (40%) will be considered for contract award.

Combined Highest Technical (60%) & Price (40%)

Proposals will be evaluated in accordance with the evaluation criteria contained in "Evaluation Criteria". Only those proposals which are compliant with all of the Mandatory Requirements and then achieve a score of sixty percent (60%) or better in EACH of the Item Rated Requirements Evaluation will be considered.

The compliant bidder with the highest combined rating technical merit (60%) and price (40%) shall be selected as the preferred supplier to undertake the Project, as exemplified in table below.

(It is clear that this Method 2 as illustrated within the section

How to Respond to a RFP
Understanding the Bid and Proposal Process

"How Price Factors into the Evaluation". The award will be based on the combination of highest technical and price evaluation. Normally this method is used when quality is more important than price. In this example, with a 40% weight on price, price has become a significant factor and almost as important as qualify.)

Note: For evaluation purpose only: the per diem will be used to determine the financial price. Should any bidder fail to meet the minimum score of any of the rated requirements, no further review will be conducted. Bidders are advised to address these requirements in the same order and in sufficient depth in their proposals. An item not addressed in the proposal will be deemed as either not meeting the criteria or given zero points under the point rated system. Proposals not meeting the requirements will not be evaluated further and will be deemed non-responsive.

Example of Best Value Determination

Bidder	Technical Points	Prices Quoted
Bidder 1	62	$1,000
Bidder 2	55	$800
Bidder 3	60	$650

Bidder	Technical Evaluation	Price Evaluation	Total Score
1	$\frac{62}{62}$ X 60 = 60.00	$\frac{650}{1000}$ X 40 = 26.00	**86.00**
2	$\frac{55}{62}$ X 60 = 53.22	$\frac{650}{800}$ X 40 = 32.50	**85.72**
3	$\frac{60}{62}$ X 60 = 58.06	$\frac{650}{650}$ X 40 = 40.00	**98.06**

(Interestingly it is now clear that this is a variation on the combination of quality and price. The Technical Bids will be compared to each other in the same way that the Price Bids will

be evaluated.)

Assumption : Three valid bids have been received. The maximum technical score that can be obtained is 70 points. The Highest technical score and lowest per diem price proposal received full rated percentage and other proposals are pro-rated accordingly.

The winner is the bidder scoring the highest total points established by adding the technical and rated price points. Based on the above calculation, a contract would be awarded to Bidder 3, which offers the highest technical score taking into consideration the technical merit and price proposal.

Should any bidder fail to meet the minimum score of any of the rated requirement, no further review will be conducted. Bidders are advised to address these requirements in the same order and in sufficient depth in their proposals. An item not addressed in the proposal will be deemed as either not meeting the criteria or given zero points under the point rated system. Proposals not meeting the requirements will not be evaluated further and will be deemed non-responsive.

1 TECHNICAL APPROACH (35 points maximum)

Demonstrated capacity to analyze in-action research instruments, as demonstrated by a description of the elements of prolongation of a project to be included in the bid. (maximum 10 points)

Demonstrated capacity to analyze research instruments, as demonstrated by a description of the elements of duplication to avoid inadvertent risk in decision making. To be included in the bid. (maximum 10 points)

Demonstrated familiarity with SQC research procurement policies. (maximum 10 points)

Demonstrated familiarity with SQC's priority areas of interest. (maximum 5 points)

2 EXPERIENCE (35 points maximum)

Demonstrated experience in project management (maximum 15 points)

Demonstrated experience in providing advice to government officials . (maximum 10 points)

Demonstrated experience in maintaining the status quo on previous related research. (maximum 10 points)

Total points 70 points maximum

SECTION "E" FINANCIAL PROPOSAL

PROJECT TITLE: STRATEGIC ADIVCE ON THE STATUS QUO

1. FINANCIAL CONTENT

The Undersigned hereby offers to Her Majesty the Queen in Right of Canada, as requested by the Minister, to furnish all necessary expertise, supervision, materials, equipment and other things necessary to the entire satisfaction of the Minister or his authorized representative, the work as described in the Request for Proposal according to the terms and conditions of the Department's Service Contract.

2. FINANCIAL PROPOSAL

(The Financial Proposal sets out the way that the costing must be presented so that all firms bid in an identical manner.)

2.1 The bidder must complete the table identified on section E, page 14 of this RFP.

Annex C
Case Study – RFP Example

The following proposal MUST be submitted **IN CANADIAN FUNDS**.

2.2 The Contractor will be paid the following firm all-inclusive per diem rate for work delivered identified below pursuant to this contract for performance of the work defined in Sections "B" Statements of Work, the Goods and Services Tax (GST) extra or Harmonized Sales Tax (HST) extra.

2.3 **Per Diem Rate** - The daily rate is based on 7.5 hours exclusive of meal breaks.

Payment shall be for actual days worked with no provision for annual leave, statutory holidays and sick leave. For work performed for a duration of more or less than one (1) day, the daily rate will be prorated accordingly to cover the actual time worked.

The Per Diem Rates must be 'all inclusive' except for travel expenses on project business outside the National Capital Region, and GST. Charges for expenses which are normally incurred in the provision of services, such as, labour for conducting negotiations and providing estimates, resolving contract disputes, tracking time sheets, monthly invoicing, facsimile, copying/printing charges, office supplies, courier, long distance telephone charges, travel from a personal residence to the SQC site in the National Capital Region, local travel and the like, must be included in the rates and will not be permitted as additional charges to contract.

3. NON-PERMANENT RESIDENT (FOREIGN CONTRACTOR)

The contractor shall ensure that non-permanent residents intending to work in Canada on a temporary basis in fulfillment of the Contract, who are neither Canadian citizens nor United States nationals, receive all appropriate documents and instructions relating to Canadian immigration requirements and secure all required employment authorizations prior to their arrival at the Canadian port of entry. The contractor shall ensure that United States nationals having such intentions receive all appropriate documents and instructions in that regard prior to their arrival at the Canadian port of entry. Such documents may be obtained at the appropriate Canadian Embassy/Consulate in the contractor's country. The contractor shall be responsible for all costs incurred as a result of non-compliance with immigration requirements.

4. TAX WITHHOLDING OF 15 PERCENT (For non-Canadian contractors only)

The contractor agrees that, pursuant to the provisions of the Income Tax Act, Canada is empowered to withhold an amount of 15 percent of the price to be paid to the contractor, if the contractor is a non-resident contractor as defined in said Act. This amount will be held on account with respect to any liability for taxes which may be owed to Canada.

5. AUDITED FINANCIAL STATEMENTS

In order to confirm a Bidder's financial capability to perform the subject requirement, the contracting authority reserves the right to have access, during the proposal evaluation phase, to current bidder financial information. If requested, the financial information to be provided shall include, but not be limited to the bidder's most recent audited financial statements or financial statements certified by the bidder's chief financial officer.

Should the bidder provide the requested information to Canada in confidence while indicating that the disclosed information is confidential, then Canada will treat the information in a confidential manner as provided in the *Access to Information Act.*

In the event that a proposal is found to be non-responsive on the basis that the bidder is considered NOT to be financially capable of performing the subject requirement, official notification shall be provided to the bidder.

6. INVOICING INSTRUCTIONS

Payment will be made 30 days after receipt of an invoice duly supported by proper documentation. The invoice must clearly state the date, contract number, the description of work and the GST number. The original and one copy of the invoice shall be forwarded to the Project Authority's attention (available upon contract award).

7.1 PROPOSED BASIS OF PAYMENT:

7.1.1 Total tendered price for the Strategic advice on Public Opinion Research is a **ceiling amount** of $75,000 plus GST in Canadian funds.

a) **Professional Services:** Bidders **must** provide the per diem rate for Professional Services as follows:
Category of Personnel:
NAME OF RESOURCE:
Per Diem Rate:
GST @ 7% or **HST** @ 15% : #

Note: Bidder shall provide his GST registration number and/or Supplier Registration information number.

8. FEDERAL GOODS AND SERVICES TAX (GST)/HARMONIZED SALES TAX (HST)

Any amount to be levied against Her Majesty in respect of the GST/HST is to be shown separately on all invoices for goods supplied or services provided and will be paid by the Government of Canada. The Contractor agrees to remit any

GST/HST paid or due to Canada Revenue Agency.

9. CLOSURE OF GOVERNMENT OFFICES

Contractor personnel are employees of the Contractor and are paid by the Contractor on the basis of services rendered. Where Contractor's employees are providing services on government premises pursuant to this Contract and the said premises become non accessible due to strike or labour stoppage, evacuation or closure of government offices, and consequently no Work is being performed as a result of the closure, Canada will not be liable for payment to the Contractor for the period of closure.

PROPOSALS WHICH DO NOT CONTAIN THE ABOVE-MENTIONED DOCUMENTATION OR WHICH DEVIATE FROM THE PRESCRIBED COSTING FORMAT MAY BE CONSIDERED INCOMPLETE AND NON-RESPONSIVE.

SECTION "F" CERTIFICATION

1. VALIDITY PERIOD

The Undersigned agree(s) that this Financial Proposal will remain firm for a period of 90 calendar days after the proposal closing date.
Signature:
Date:

2. BIDDER CERTIFICATION

'We hereby certify that all information provided herein is accurate. Furthermore we have satisfied ourselves that the personnel proposed by us for this requirement are capable of satisfactorily performing the requirement described herein. In addition, we certify that individuals proposed will be available until completion of the project. Also that the work specified herein can be met in a timely manner, and will be achieved within the time frame allocated.'

As well, by affixing an authorized Company official signature hereunder, the bidder confirms acceptance in its entirety of the Professional Services Contracting Terms and Conditions applicable to this requirement.

Signature of Authorized Company Official:
Date:

3. PRICE CERTIFICATION

The bidder certifies that the price quoted in this proposal is not in excess of the lowest price charged to anyone else, including its most favored customer, for like quality and quantity of the products/services, does not include an element of profit on the sale in excess of that normally obtained by the bidder on the sale of products/services of like quality and quantity, and does not include any provision for discounts to selling agents.

Signature:
Date:

4. EDUCATION / EXPERIENCE:

"We hereby certify that all statements made with regard to the education and the experience of individuals proposed for completing the subject work are accurate and factual, and we are aware that Status Quo Canada reserves the right to verify any information provided in this regard and that untrue statements may result in the proposal being declared non-responsive or in other action which the Minister may consider appropriate."

Signature:
Date:

5. CERTIFICATION OF AVAILABILITY AND STATUS OF PERSONNEL:

5.1 Availability of Personnel: The Bidder certifies that, should it be authorized to provide services under any Contract resulting from this solicitation, the persons proposed in its bid will be available to commence performance of the work immediately upon contract award and will remain available to perform the work in relation to the fulfillment of this requirement".

5.2 Status of Personnel: "If the bidder has proposed any person in fulfillment of this requirement who is not an employee of the bidder, the bidder hereby certifies that it has written permission from such person (or the employer of such person) to propose the services of such person in relation to the work to be performed in fulfillment of this requirement and to submit such person's résumé to the Contracting Authority. As well, the bidder hereby certifies that the proposed person is aware that overtime may be required and is willing to comply."

Signature:
Date:

6. FEDERAL CONTRACTOR PROGRAM FOR EMPLOYMENT EQUITY (over $25,000 and under $200,000)

6.1 Organizations that are subject to the Federal Contractors Program for Employment Equity (FCP-EE) but that have been declared ineligible to receive government contracts of goods and services over the threshold for solicitation of bids as set out in the Government Contract Regulations (GCRs) (currently $25,000 including applicable taxes), either as a result of a finding of noncompliance by SQC-Labour, or following their voluntary withdrawal from the FCP-EE) for a reason other than a reduction in their workforce, have been advised by SQC-Labour that as a consequence of this action they are no longer eligible to receive any government contract over this threshold. Consequently, their

Annex C
Case Study – RFP Example

certificate numbers have been cancelled and their names have been placed on SQC-Labour's List of Ineligible Contractors. Bids from such organizations will be considered non-responsive.

6.2 The bidder is required to certify that it has not been declared "ineligible" by SQC-Labour to receive government contracts over the GCRs threshold for solicitation of bids (currently $25,000) as a result of a finding of non-compliance, or as a result of having voluntarily withdrawn from the FCP-EE for a reason other than a reduction in their workforce.

Signature of authorized representative:
Date:

6.3 The bidder acknowledges that the Minister shall rely on this certification to award the contract. Should a verification by the Minister disclose a misrepresentation on the part of the bidder, the Minister shall have the right to treat any contract resulting from this bid as being in default.

Note: Contractors that have been declared "Ineligible Contractors" are no longer eligible to receive government contracts over the threshold for solicitation of bids as set out in the Government Contract Regulations (currently at $25,000), either as a result of a finding of non-compliance by SQC-Labour, or following their voluntary withdrawal from the Program for a reason other than the reduction in their workforce. Any bid from ineligible contractors will not be considered for award.

The bidder is required to certify to its status with as follows:

The bidder,
a.(   ) is not subject to FCP-EE, having a workforce of less than 100 persons in Canada,
b.(   ) is not subject to FCP-EE, being a regulated employer under the Employment Equity Act;
c.(   ) is subject to the requirements of FCP-EE, having a

workforce of 100 persons or more, but has not previously obtained a certificate number from SQC-Labour, (having not bid on requirements of $200,000 or more), in which case a duly signed certificate of commitment is provided herewith (attached);
d.(   ) is subject to FCP-EE, and has a valid certification number as follows: _____ (e.g. has not been declared "Ineligible Contractor" by SQC-Labour).

Signature of authorized representative:
Date:

If the bidder does not fall within the exceptions enumerated in 2. (a) or (b), the Program requirements do apply, and as such, the bidder is required to submit a Certificate of Commitment DULY SIGNED as referenced below or a valid Certificate number confirming its adherence to the FCP-EE.

The bidder acknowledges that the Minister shall rely on this certification to award the contract. Should a verification by the Minister disclose a misrepresentation on the part of the bidder, the Minister shall have the right to treat any contract resulting from this bid as being in default. In all cases, the bidder is required to produce evidence or supporting information on demand prior to contract award, if such evidence is not included with its bid.

SECTION "G" INTELLECTUAL PROPERTY

Intellectual Property clauses are available on the following internet link:

Basis for Canada's Ownership of Intellectual Property (Re: 7.1)
(g) The Crown has opted to own the Intellectual Property Rights in Foreground Information which consists of material subject to copyright except computer software or any documentation pertaining to such software.

RED TEAM REVIEW OF RFP

(The following is to illustrate the format and methodology of a Red Team review. As stated earlier in the book, the Red Team NEVER edits the proposal. The same is said of the RFP. You will note as the Red Team comments on an RFP, the Red Team raises questions that should be submitted to the Contracting Authority. While the following comments reference the RFP, the same format is used for each evaluation of Proposal drafts.)

"STRATEGIC ADVICE ON MAINTAINING THE STATUS QUO"

Q1.
Solicitation Closing Time is September 31, 2008. There is no September 31, 2012.. Please advise correct closing time.

(Section A, Proposal Instructions, clause 3 c) states "submit a proposal no more than 10 pages in length." There is a lack of clarity. Spacing (single, double, etc. is missing, margins need to be defined (top, bottom, side to side) and font size. This leaves it open to firms to "shrink" the written component or enlarge the room that can be written on to expand their proposal size.)

Q2.
Section A, Proposal Instructions, clause 3c) states "submit a proposal no more than 10 pages in length." In order to ensure consistency of proposals between bidders, please advise page margins, font size and spacing of writing (single, 1 1/3, double space).

Section A, Proposal Instructions, clause 5. Revisions – this is not clear.

Q3.
Please advise the meaning of Clause 5. It would appear to be a extension of clause 12. Bidder Suggestions During the Period of

the RFP.

Q4.
Section A. Proposal Instructions, clause 10.1 states that it is "the Contractor's responsibility to completely understand the requirements…"

Is there an existing contractor already performing the service?

Q5.
Section A. Proposal Instructions, clause 12: Clause 11 is missing. Please advise if this is an oversight or just misnumbering of clauses.

Q6.
Section D. Evaluation Criteria: The Rated Evaluation is 60% and the Price is 40%. Our experience is that price is normally not in excess of 25%. We would ask that this be amended to reflect a more appropriate balance.

Q7.
Section D, Evaluation Criteria, clause 1. Technical Approach, 1st line.

Please advise how project management relates to the requirement of maintaining the status quo.

(There are other questions that could be asked. For illustration purposes the above will suffice. These questions are forwarded to the Proposal Manager. This individual has to decide if the question is to be submitted to the procurement officer. It may be that the answer is already known. It could also be desirable not to let potential competitor know of gaps in the bidder's knowledge.)

Annex D

Professional Resume – Allan Cutler

Mr. Allan Cutler has over 30 years' experience in the public and private sector. During his career, he managed multi-million dollar complex and sensitive procurements being responsible for the successful evaluation, award and contract administration until the expiry of the contracts. He is skilled in troubleshooting with a demonstrated capacity to achieve results.

He has participated in developing Statements of Work and evaluation criteria for bid documents, which have been uniquely structured. He also assists firms in reviewing and in developing compliant proposals in response to competitive bid solicitations.

Allan Cutler also is a noted trainer and consultant in procurement and ethics. Presently he offers courses in Ethical Procurement, Negotiation Strategies, How to Respond to a Request for Proposal and Organizational Ethics. He is a frequent speaker on various ethical topics such as whistleblowing and organizational ethics.

Allan Cutler is also known as the "Whistleblower" from his involvement in trying to stop the abuses that resulted in the Sponsorship Scandal.

PRESENTATIONS
- Meeting Planners International, "Ethical Negotiation"
- Saskatchewan Crown Corporations, "Whistleblowing"
- 7th Annual Alliance for Excellence in Investigative and Forensic Accounting Conference, Whistleblowing

- The 8th Annual Ottawa Chapter Fraud Professionals' Conference, Whistleblowing
- Carleton University and St. Paul's University, "Whistleblowing and the Sponsorship Scandal".

TRAINING
- Ethical Procurement and Sustainability
- Negotiation Strategies
- How to Respond to an RFP
- Organizational Ethics

OTHER ACTIVITIES
- Advisor, Algonquin College, e-Business Supply Chain Management Advisory Committee
- Member, Materiel Management Institute
- Member, The Ethics Practitioner's Association of Canada
- Member, Transparency International
- President, Canadians for Accountability

AWARDS:
To The Top Canada Award, January , 2006. This is an award to recognize a Canadian who through their individual effort has made Canada a better place.

Five Who Made a Difference, January, 2006. The Ottawa Sun salutes Allan Cutler for making a difference to Ottawa "Government/Politics" in 2005.

One of the Top 50 People in Ottawa – 2005. Ottawa Life magazine

CONTACT INFORMATION:
Allan Cutler
E-mail: ascutler@ascutler.com